MINDFUL *Magnetic* WOMAN

UNDERSTANDING THE LEVELS OF REAL ATTRACTIVENESS TO MAXIMIZE YOUR INNER AND OUTER GLOW

Beautyrobic.

www.beautyrobic.com

ISBN: 978-615-01-6343-7 (hardcover)
ISBN: 978-615-01-5688-0 (audiobook)

Original title: WOW HATÁS Fedezd fel a Valódi Vonzeröd © 2018
The translation is based on the WOW HATÁS 5th. extended edition 2022
Translated by: Zsuzsanna László, Márta Fogarasi

MINDFUL *Magnetic* WOMAN

UNDERSTANDING THE LEVELS
OF REAL ATTRACTIVENESS TO MAXIMIZE
YOUR INNER AND OUTER GLOW

BRIGITTA BEKESI

TABLE *of* CONTENTS

PREFACE

Once upon a time, there was a little girl who was not very pretty or very smart.

There were times when her appearance was ridiculed at school, and she was considered a mediocre student. She was put on a wait list to get into high school and teachers didn't encourage her much there either. In a small room of a 10-story blockhouse in Budapest, this mousy little wallflower dreamed about how it would all be different one day. Every night, she imagined finding the love of her life and being a special, successful, attractive and happy woman that everyone loved.

The story isn't unusual so far, but two strong elements changed everything.

The girl never lost sight of her determination or the belief that something better existed.

Deep down, she believed that one day she would show the world that she was better than this. And not only did she believe it, she worked hard to make it a reality.

The girl started working out, learned what types of clothes looked good on her, and studied hard—much harder than others, because she had to. In her free time, while others were watching TV and having fun, she was reading books and improving herself. She would work a job after school because she didn't want to have less than her classmates. In the end, it was that job that led her to her true love, and she was on a full scholarship by the time she finished school.

When she graduated, she continued working. But, deep down, she knew she wanted more, so she didn't stop learning and became an entrepreneur. At 6 pm, when everyone finished work and went to rest, she would go to her business and continue working there late into the night. She also worked on the weekends, training herself to become more than before. It was a very hard period of her life, with many busy days and dead-tired evenings. And when her first business went bankrupt, everyone discouraged her from trying again.

But she refused to give up on her dreams. It took a lot of perseverance, courage, work, time and self-education to keep her going. But the hard work eventually paid off.

Today, she is at the point where she doesn't need to work for anyone else. She has her own company, which she adores and improves every day. She inspires a lot of women in her business. She gets a ton of messages from clients about how her and her method has changed their lives by making them feel sexy and charismatic. She makes a living helping others become happier and more attractive. What's more, she and her husband are still very much in love, after 20 years together.

I could finish this fairytale by saying, "And they lived happily ever after…" but by now I'm sure you know that this story is *my* story.

So, if you're wondering how I know my method works, it's because I am the living example of it. And those who know me personally are amazed at how much I've changed over time. Since I've walked this path, I'm perfectly aware that it's not easy, and requires a lot of work and energy. But I also know that if you put your mind to it, you will make it. If I managed to succeed, you can too.

People rarely make rational decisions even if they think they do. Most of our decisions are unconscious and based on emotion. Even during big decisions, when we think we are being logical, we seem only to create rational explanations for our emotional decisions.

Relationships, whether business or personal, are successful when you become the type of person who can positively influence others emotionally. No matter what area of life it may be—love, social interactions, business relationships and so on—whether you will have an impact on others depends on you. Whether or not you will be trusted by others, or manage to persuade others, whether someone will want to commit to you, and or want to associate with you, it all depends on you.

How successful you are and what you achieve in life depends on how many people you positively impact and make an impression on—basically, how many people think, "She is amazing!" when thinking about you!

My purpose with this book is to show you how to maximize your inner and outer glow, how to become more attractive, charismatic, and confident in yourself, and how to attract people to you so they pay attention to what you say and do and find you to be special and magnetic. I want to unleash your magnetic potential and for people to think one thing when they think of you: "WOW"!

If there is a power capable of changing your life, this is it!

chapter one

INTRODUCTION TO L.O.R.A.

LEVELS OF REAL ATTRACTIVENESS

I have always been interested in helping women empower themselves to feel attractive and have the inner glow that brings them confidence, success and happiness. To help other women, I've worked as a professional life coach, a fitness trainer and a yoga instructor. To add to my knowledge in these areas, I've studied naturopathy, nutrition, phytotherapy, tantra, face yoga, and manual techniques like massage, myofascial release, and energy release.

With all the knowledge I compiled, I was able to design and

develop my very own program to empower women's bodies and minds. In 2012, my program Beautyrobic[1] went on the market and has since become a huge success in Hungary.

When I first started Beautyrobic, I wanted to create a hard, effective, but feminine workout. In the beginning, the focus was mainly on body shaping, but I realized Beautyrobic had so much more potential, which led me to expand its focus outside the physical body.

Thousands of women have improved their lives with Beautyrobic—whether their health, posture, body shape, self-confidence, femininity, self-love, general well-being, or overall happiness. My program has gained national recognition in Hungary; I was awarded a "Promise for the Future" award by the Young Entrepreneurs Association and asked to speak for TEDx about the three forgotten ingredients of attractiveness.[2] I enjoyed the progress I was making, but I wanted to help even more women.

My team and I started by surveying numerous men and women to ask what attractiveness meant to them, and what made someone interesting, charming or magnetic. Nearly everyone associated attractiveness with an "inner glow" or a radiant inner beauty. But

---

1 Beautyrobic is a special workout where, apart from body-shaping, health, and weight loss goals, we emphasize femininity, sensuality, self-love, self-esteem and confidence. Our mission and purpose is to help women feel alluring, feminine, confident and healthy inside and out. We help them to maximize their inner and outer glow. Beautyrobic has become a women's lifestyle brand where, as well as special workouts, we provide meditation, tutorials, online/offline courses, workshops, trainings, and other programs. The effectiveness of Beautyrobic has been proven by thousands of women— with regular practice, they have made positive change, both physically and mentally.

2 Brigitta Békési, "A vonzerő 3 elfeledett összetevője" filmed December 17, 2019 in Győr, Hungary, TedxTalks, 17:49, https://youtu.be/HsgNee36nRM.

the more interesting revelation was yet to come.

We also asked the respondents what they did when they were feeling less attractive for some reason, e.g., they had broken up with their significant other or had been going through an emotional rough patch. Nearly everyone tried to increase their own attractiveness by looking for some solution associated with physical appearance. They went to the hairdresser, started going to the gym or began a diet.

I wondered why people almost unanimously thought that an inner glow made someone else attractive, but when they wanted to become attractive themselves, they started working out, bought new clothes, got a new hairdo or perhaps even saw a plastic surgeon. They made changes on a physical level, but not at the level where they might get an inner glow. Why is that?

I concluded that most people have absolutely no clue what makes them attractive to those around them. They spoke about inner glow and self-confidence, but since they didn't know how to maximize their own magnetism, they used completely different methods of achieving attractiveness when it came to themselves. They changed their looks, hoping that this would make them attractive and interesting. But that is not enough to achieve their magnetic potential.

If that were truly enough, why are so many beautiful people unhappy or unsuccessful? And how come people whose physical appearance is far from perfect have huge success?

The answer is simple: physical perfection is not enough to achieve Real Attractiveness! Clearly, being attractive is not merely about physical appearance, so we must seek new solutions.

People often mistakenly think that successful people are more attractive because of their wealth, and that that's the secret to success in their personal lives as well. But that's not true! The attitude that makes you successful in business is the same attitude that makes you charming and interesting to others; if you adopt this attitude, well, you will have success and happiness in both your personal and professional life.

This book is the physical manifestation of extensive interviews and more than a decade of experience with Beautyrobic combined with my own business knowledge, which I have gained both through running my business and studying as an economist. This experience informed my creation of a system that everybody will be able to understand and, more importantly, use, to maximize their Real Attractiveness and become a Mindful Magnetic Woman. This book presents the system, outlining what Real Attractiveness means, its levels, how each level can be achieved, and what resources and techniques are available in order to maximize your inner and outer glow and attract the life you deserve.

Imagine this as your grandma's secret cake recipe.

If you want to bake this cake from memory, you may not know the exact ingredients, quantities, proportions and baking method to use. You may forget something, add too much or too little of an ingredient or select the wrong baking time. The point is that you would only be guessing, which will have a negative impact on the outcome. However, if you have the exact recipe and steps, you will know how to reproduce granny's special treat that you loved nibbling on as a kid. All you have to do is follow the perfect recipe!

This book explains, in detail, the levels of Real Attractiveness and gives you practical advice on how to achieve them. If you follow what's written, your life will change. In other words: I'm giving you the recipe for becoming a Mindful Magnetic Woman!

Of course, every person is attractive to somebody, but if you become a Mindful Magnetic Woman, you will experience improvement in your quality of life. You will feel the impact of this book in both your personal and professional life, because every deal, job interview or promotion is the result of a decision-maker giving you a vote of confidence.

I am certain that all of us have seen decisions be made based on someone's personality rather than their merits. If two people apply for the same job and one has all the right credentials but lacks confidence and seems unfriendly, and the other is not fully qualified but is charismatic, magnetic and engaging, the charismatic person is more likely to get the job. They are more attractive to employers because they can bring positivity to the company. Now, imagine how many areas of life you can win in if you dazzle people with your charm and maximize your inner and outer glow!

THE SYSTEM

Levels of Real Attractiveness (L.O.R.A.)

I have created a five-level system for attractiveness.

Through the levels, you can become more and more empowered as a woman. Age is not a factor! You can become so alluring that you sweep others off their feet. You can unlock your inner and outer glow and maximize them! This is what I want for you.

Think of Real Attractiveness as a rose. A woman who has nothing but her looks is like a rosebud that never bursts into bloom. In her twenties, her beauty and looks might carry her through; a rosebud can be very beautiful. But there's nothing sadder than when time passes and a flower does not bloom or grow. In contrast, a woman who finds her Real Attractiveness and slowly fulfills herself is like a flower gracefully unfolding, gradually revealing a wonderful, complex beauty. The layers of unfolding petals show that what is on the inside is more powerful and beautiful than that closed little bud. That woman becomes magnetically attractive and irresistibly charismatic. That woman becomes a Mindful Magnetic Woman and more successful in all the different areas of her life!

It is important to note that attractiveness is not something you achieve once, and then check off your list without having to do anything else. The different levels of attractiveness require effort on a <u>daily</u> basis. Just as you need to exercise regularly to stay in shape, the same applies to becoming alluring, attractive and magnetic.

The choice is yours! If you want to work hard towards becoming attractive, you can achieve it!

I call this five-level system **L.o.R.A.**, or **L**evels **of R**eal **A**ttractiveness.

The levels build upon one another. Like building a house, special attention must be given to every phase of the process. If a house is not built on a solid foundation, it will collapse. That is why I ask you to start from the lowest level and work up to the highest level. If you follow all the exercises in this book, you will get there. Just give yourself time and be patient.

Like rose petals unfurling into full bloom, start with Level 1 and then expand into each level.

We will discuss each level and complete practical exercises. After completing each exercise, you will acquire the skills relevant to each level. If necessary, you may read the chapters several times.

Give yourself time! As you progress, you will become more

and more charming, charismatic and magnetic. The more levels you complete, the harder it will be to replace you, and the more profound and more timeless your Real Attractiveness will be!

"They can conquer who believe they can."

—Virgil[3]

---

3 Dryden, *The Works of Virgil, Volume 3* (London: Forgotten Books, 2017): 101.

chapter two

LEVEL I: APPEARANCE

MIRROR, MIRROR...

W hen we delve into the topic of attractiveness, we find that outward appearance is not the most important factor, but it *does* matter, and it makes an impression on others. There are countless examples of people succeeding in their endeavors mainly because they are more attractive than their peers. To see this, all you need to do is take a look at the number of followers some attractive girls have on Instagram or observe how men approach physically attractive women in a club or at a party.

Today, more and more people are using the Internet and dating apps to find a potential partner. This means that who we are interested in will primarily depend on a profile picture and a few short lines in their profile. This also means that a woman with an attractive physical appearance has a competitive advantage in the dating marketplace.

This advantage is not limited to just choosing a partner. In the U.S., psychologists have coined the term "the beauty premium" to describe this phenomenon.[4] A study done for the *Journal of Vocational Behavior* examined how the beauty premium works.[5] The study followed 203 adults after they graduated from college programs and started their careers. It followed them for two years and discovered that those who were more physically attractive were granted higher starting salaries and were given access to more resources at the start of their careers than those deemed less attractive. Right from the start, those that were seen as more attractive were also given more exposure and visibility in their careers. This gave them a strong advantage from the time they entered the workforce.

Besides the workplace and dating, an attractive appearance can be an advantage socially. There was an interesting experiment conducted where two women carried a heavy suitcase up the stairs.[6] One of them was considered an attractive woman, while the other was average looking. It only took four seconds before a man approached the physically attractive woman to offer her help, but 45 seconds before two other women offered to help the

---

4   Karyn Dossinger, Connie R. Wanberg, Yongjun Choi, and Lisa M. Leslie, "The beauty premium: The role of organizational sponsorship in the relationship between physical attractiveness and early career salaries," *Journal of Vocational Behavior* 112 (June 2019): 109.

5   Ibid.

6   "The Halo Effect," HeroicImaginationTV, YouTube, September 25, 2011, https://youtu.be/UEho_4ejkNw.

average-looking woman. This scenario was repeated several times to ensure that the first result was not just a fluke. Overall, the physically attractive woman was approached on average after 8 seconds, while it took an average of 24 seconds for the average-looking woman to be approached.

By 1960, television had become part of mass media in the U.S. It was the year of the first televised presidential debate between candidates Richard M. Nixon and John F. Kennedy. The younger and more inexperienced John F. Kennedy clearly won over the television viewers, while Nixon won over those listening to the debate on the radio. The explanation for this result is that Kennedy, quite simply, looked better on TV.[7] Nixon had just gotten out of the hospital. He had lost weight, seemed exhausted and tense, and seemed generally unwell. Over the radio, where the audience could only hear the candidates, the more experienced Nixon came across as more authoritative, but this was insufficient to win the presidency against the millions of television viewers who voted for Kennedy.[8]

It is clear that outward appearance does matter in various areas of life. This is not just a result of the supposedly superficial world we live in. Beauty and physical attractiveness inspire trust.[9] But I do have good news for you. All the experts I interviewed throughout my research, regardless of their field of expertise,

---

[7] "How the Kennedy-Nixon Debate Changed the World of Politics," *Constitution Daily*, September 26, 2017, https://constitutioncenter.org/blog/the-debate-that-changed-the-world-of-politics.

[8] Ibid.

[9] Na Zhao, Yuanyuan Shi, Mingjie Zhou, and Jianxin Zhang, "Face Attractiveness in Building Trust: Evidence from Measurement of Implicit and Explicit Responses," *Social Behavior and Personality: An International Journal* 43, no 5 (June 2015): 855. http://dx.doi.org/10.2224/sbp.2015.43.5.855.

mentioned one common recurring element: if you take care of yourself and dedicate time and attention to your appearance, it can be improved. This is best said by Helena Rubinstein: "There are no ugly women in the world, only lazy ones."[10] This has never been truer than in this day and age.

But, if physical attractiveness has such a great power, then why is it only Level 1—that is, the first and most basic of the Levels of Real Attractiveness?

It's easy to attract someone's attention to you with beauty alone, but it is just as easy to lose someone's attention if there is nothing else behind it. Eventually, someone more attractive will come along, or people will tire of seeing the same empty beauty and will want something different or deeper. Remember: men who seek nothing more than youth and beauty in a woman will inevitably seek out an even younger and more beautiful woman. Admittedly, looks are an important factor in overall attractiveness, but they are far from being the most important quality.

Being attractive is attainable for anyone, but it isn't free. Often a young girl with good genes will think that she can do whatever she wants—eat junk food, not sleep, and drink excessive amounts of alcohol—without the effects showing on her skin. Believe me, and I speak from experience, when you are young, your skin really does not reveal your lifestyle, but in 10 years' time, the signs will appear.

The difference between two 30-year-old women can be dramatic depending on how much care they dedicate to themselves. A 30-year-old may look like a 20-year-old, but she may also look

---

10 Laura Regensdorf, "'There Are No Ugly Women, Only Lazy Ones': A New Beauty Exhibition Explores the Life and Legacy of Helena Rubinstein," *Vogue*, October 31, 2014, https://www.vogue.com/slideshow/helena-rubinstein-beauty-cosmetics-jewish-museum-exhibition.

10–15 years older. The foundation of how you age is laid as early as your 20s. However, once you are over 40, these differences can become more pronounced and increasingly apparent to the naked eye. The shocking thing is that your appearance can not only show how much water you drink and how you treat your body and skin, but also how happy and balanced your life is.

Facial features, such as the down-turned, drooping corners of the mouth, deep creases, or wrinkles on your face tell the tale of your previous life experience, and this is closely correlated to your charisma. A woman over 40 can look stunning if her lifestyle allows it.

Let's go over exactly what you will need to consider when it comes to an attractive appearance. I have divided appearance into two categories: **face** and **body.**

Face:

▸ Skincare

▸ Makeup

▸ Hairstyle

Body:

▸ Nutrition

▸ Exercise

▸ Movement

▸ Posture

▸ Flexibility

▸ Clothing and style

Before you dive into the subject, you must ask yourself these two very important questions:

Who are you really? What is the message that you wish to convey about yourself?

Your whole image, the picture that you show to the external world, must be based on this response. **This picture must align with your inner self, otherwise you will come across as fake and people will perceive you as such, which is not attractive.**

Just think of a woman wearing a pair of heels that she looks uncomfortable wearing. High heels can be incredibly sexy, but on a woman who is struggling to wear them, they can look unnatural or even comical. If you want to be truly attractive, do not follow the latest fashion trends or wear what you think you "should." Instead, find a style that is in harmony with your personality.

Every expert I interviewed, regardless of their field of expertise, agreed on one thing: the most important thing to consider when changing your look is to tailor it to *your* personality and style. In addition, you need to align these changes with your current lifestyle and activities!

Always remember to ask yourself:

Who am I really? What is the message I wish to convey about myself?

FACE

MAKEUP

Let's talk about makeup first. I love red lipstick and I think I can pull it off. But I won't tell you that if you want to be attractive you should rock a red lip, because it may not suit your personality or look flattering on you. Perhaps my favorite lipstick shade is not flattering on you, but another shade looks gorgeous. Or perhaps the timing for you to rock a red lip or other makeup trend may not be right. What I mean is that what flatters us best changes with age. Just because something looks great on you at 20, it might not when you are 50.

That's precisely the reason why there isn't a hard-and-fast rule everyone should live by; it is more like an art. You can experiment, and you should! Go on the Internet, check out social media posts, watch YouTube makeup videos, and try out new techniques for applying your makeup. Draw inspiration from these sources and try new things. The key is to draw inspiration from others, rather than directly emulating them, and adapt everything based on your personality and personal style.

However, there are some universal beauty tips that every girl should know. For instance, be sure to choose the right foundation shade for your skin tone, and when shopping for foundation, test the shade on your face rather than your hand or wrist, since your face might be an entirely different color.

If you want to apply makeup like a pro, take my advice and invest some time, energy, and yes, money to hire a professional makeup artist. Professional, perfectly applied makeup will not act like a mask but will enhance your beauty and natural features while also concealing any flaws like scars or skin blemishes. Makeup is an amazing way to express your personality and look beautiful for any occasion. Learning from a professional and getting their recommendation is usually cheaper than buying all sorts of useless, unnecessary beauty products that won't work for you. I don't know about you, but I have a staggering amount of makeup products I bought, used once, and never used again.

If you want to avoid this vicious cycle, you will want to

adopt a more conscious approach to your makeup. Don't fall for the commercials and hype, instead try to express your **unique personality!**

Here are the top 5 makeup tips I think every woman should know:

1. Find a good foundation that matches your skin type and skin color. Be careful because your skin color can change in different seasons; skin can be darker in summer from suntanning, then lighter in winter.

2. It is worth investing in a high-quality makeup brush set.

3. Choose a lipstick that fits your skin tone. With the right color, your teeth will look whiter and brighter.

4. Don't go anywhere without a high-quality mascara.

5. Try to choose products that are organic, animal friendly, and good for your skin and the environment.

extra gift

For more information about makeup, you will find my interview with world-class makeup artist at the link below:

www.mindfulmagneticwoman.com/gift

SKINCARE

Skincare provides the foundation for flawless makeup application. The more you take care of your skin, the fewer flaws you will feel the need to cover with makeup.

In my experience, there is no skincare product, no matter how expensive or what its advertisement claims, that can solve the problems caused by inadequate nutrition, sleep deprivation, excessive stress or insufficient hydration.

That is why I am asking you to devote particular attention to the following steps:

▸ Always make sure you are drinking enough water, or some tea that will benefit your body such as rooibos, white, green, or herbal.

▸ Get at least seven hours of sleep a night, but preferably eight.

▸ Cut down on alcohol and coffee.

▸ Pay attention to your nutrition. Make sure you eat an adequate diet personalized to your needs. If you suspect you may have a food allergy, get yourself tested, and always remember to eat enough fruits and veggies.

▸ Try to reduce the stress in your life as much as possible.

▸ Laugh more! Enjoy a good laugh as often as you can. Spend your time with people who inspire you and do activities that truly energize you.

Perhaps you are still young and haven't experienced the effect that your lifestyle may have on your body. Believe me, in a few years you will see it in the quality of your skin! It is only a matter of time; sooner or later, everyone's skin will reveal the life they have been leading.

Our skin is the largest organ in our body, and it is always visible, so we should protect it and care for its beauty and health.[11] I believe the best way to help you take care of it is to teach you to think for yourself and arrive at an informed, responsible decision. I apply the same approach to choosing the right cosmetic products and building an appropriate personalized skincare routine for your skin type. I highly suggest you consult a specialist to know your own skin type better and be sure what is good for your own skin— skin can be dry, oily, sensitive, etc. Each type has different care requirements, and your skin type can change with your lifestyle and age. I will repeat myself from the makeup section by saying that learning from a professional and getting their recommendation is usually cheaper than buying all sorts of useless, unnecessary beauty products that won't work for you.

The saying, "All that glitters is not gold" is especially true for cosmetics! No matter how fancy the packaging or amazing the commercial is, or whether you find the product on the shelves of every supermarket and drug store or only in exclusive boutiques, none of this can guarantee that the product is actually good for your skin.

But there is something that never lies, and it appears on every product because it is a legal requirement. It speaks volumes and reveals more than any advertisement. It is the INCI list!

What is INCI?

INCI: the cosmetic label on the packaging containing the

---

11 Kim Ann Zimmermann, "Skin: The Human Body's Largest Organ," Live Science, October 22, 2018, https://www.livescience.com/27115-skin-facts-diseases-conditions.html.

list of chemical ingredients of the product. INCI stands for "International Nomenclature of Cosmetic Ingredients."

If you look at any cosmetic product in the store, you will find this list on it. Legislation requires that this information be provided to consumers. If you learn to read the INCI list, or rather to analyze and understand it, you will know what a cosmetic product consists of and you will no longer have to wonder which one to purchase. This allows you to make a conscious and informed decision. Do not be afraid: you don't need to become a chemist to understand the ingredients list of INCI. In Google and other search engines you can find all the information you need about the ingredients.

Luckily, there is a lot of information available on the Internet from skincare experts (dermatologists, beauticians, bloggers) so you can learn more about this topic. I want you to know what you put on your skin and be more aware when you spend your money on cosmetics and different aesthetic treatments.

It is worth it, because a good skincare routine and the right treatments can keep your skin beautiful and let it glow for years to come.

Here are my top 5 tips skincare I think every woman should know:

1. In skincare, regularity is key. Have a good skincare routine daily.

2. Always check the INCI, which shows the list of ingredients.

3. What is good for one person can be bad for another. Always test the products on yourself.

4. SPF is a must in the daytime if you want to avoid wrinkles.

5. Try to choose products that are organic, animal friendly, and good for your skin and the environment.

extra gift

For more information about skincare, you will find my interview with skincare expert at the link below:

www.mindfulmagneticwoman.com/gift

HAIR

Just like wearing the wrong makeup on your face can be unflattering, the same goes for picking your hair color or haircut. There are plenty of factors that influence what hairstyle is best for you—and trust me, among the many variables, the latest trend is the last thing that matters.

Important factors to consider when choosing a hairstyle are your face shape, skin tone, eye color, and eyebrow color. The texture of your hair will also play an essential part, as well as your lifestyle. (For example, regular swimmers may find extremely long hair or extensions annoying or too high maintenance.)

I strongly discourage you from box dyeing your hair at home or treating it at home in general. Place your trust in a professional. Choose an expert who is really interested in getting to know you and is not on the lookout for someone to experiment on. Look for a hairstylist who considers the best hairstyle for you based on your individual characteristics and whose primary focus is to find what truly complements you!

Don't forget to ask yourself the questions I cannot stress enough:

Who am I really? What is the message that I wish to convey about myself?

It's fun to look at the hottest trends and the latest celebrity hairstyles but only use their hair as a source of inspiration. Just like with makeup, I recommend you watch some YouTube videos for some useful tips and advice. Other sites I recommend for inspiration are Pinterest and TikTok, where you can find amazing hair braiding techniques and tutorials! These resources are so helpful because the more inspiration you have, the more options you have for choosing the perfect look for you.

Here are my top 5 tips I think every woman should know.

1. Use professional haircare products.

2. Nourish your hair from the inside with hair supplements

and collagen.

3. Get your hair cut regularly.

4. If you heat your hair, use heat protection products.

5. It's a must to find a good quality hairbrush.

extra gift

For more information about hair styling, you will find my interview with hair stylist at the link below:

www.mindfulmagneticwoman.com/gift

HOMEWORK

▶ Browse YouTube and TikTok videos and for one week every day, do your makeup and hair based on the inspiration you find in the videos.

▶ Look for some credible skincare experts on the Internet and start to follow them. Watch some of their videos, tutorials, or posts and start to learn more about this topic.

BODY

NUTRITION

We are all overwhelmed by articles about new diet crazes in magazines and on the Internet, day after day. Many of us fall into the trap of trying one or more of these too-good-to-be-true, unbelievably unhealthy dietary plans. These diets promise you a quick fix and drastic changes in just a few days. These are crazy solutions for people who are desperate to lose weight.

I'm sure you are fed up with celebrity crash diets that overpromise and under-deliver. Perhaps they do produce results initially, but are ultimately unsuccessful in keeping off the weight in the long run. This process can lead to yo-yo dieting and make things even worse. It may even put your body at risk for health issues. These diets don't lead to high-quality weight loss.[12] Fortunately, more and more people are beginning to realize this and recognize that crash diets will never produce a real solution.

What is the right way to have the body of your dreams?

I believe that knowledge is power! If you dedicate the time to study up and understand how your body and digestion works, and what really starts fat loss, you will not fall prey to catchy marketing. Instead, you will be able to work out a sensible nutrition plan that really works for you. Healthy eating alone is a topic that deserves a separate book, which is why it is very worthwhile for you to study up on it. Healthy eating is the foundation of our health

---

12 Shilpa Joshi and Viswanathan Mohan, "Pros and Cons of Some Popular Extreme Weight-Loss Diets," *The Indian Journal of Medical Research* 148, vol. 5 (November 2018): 642, https://www.doi.org/10.4103/ijmr. IJMR_1793_18.

and contributes to a shapely, fit and healthy body! There is no point in constantly working out or using a ton of beauty tricks if your nutrition is inadequate. Sooner or later, poor nutrition will negatively impact not only your figure, but also your skin, hair and your appearance as a whole.

A healthy body is:
70% nutrition
30% exercise[13]

Once you have learned how to eat a proper diet and get the fat loss process started, you will still have a very important task to tackle. You can't skip this if you want to succeed.

Find a nutrition regimen that suits your lifestyle, genetics, and personal taste so well that you can incorporate it into your life for the long haul—CONSISTENTLY!

I realized that the reason people often cannot achieve results with respect to nutrition is that they completely disregard the fact that **their eating habits must suit their lifestyle**. There are plenty of foods, diet plans, and programs you can choose from, which is a great thing, but if they don't suit your preferences, lifestyle, budget

---

13 Heather Jackson, "The 70/30 Rule: Breaking Down the Old School Weight Loss Plan," Fitness 19, February 25, 2015, https://www.fitness19.com/the-7030-rule-breaking-down-the-old-school-weight-loss-plan/.

or daily routine, you won't be able to stick with it for the long run. It is important to consider genetics in your diet as well, such as a family history of high cholesterol or heart disease. One of the secrets to having an amazing body is staying **consistent** with your healthy eating habits.

You must develop dietary habits that are truly sustainable for the long run!

To do this, I recommend you answer these questions first:

- ▸ Do you have a sweet tooth, or resist sweets easily?
- ▸ Do you eat meat and milk products?
- ▸ Do you have any food intolerances or allergies?
- ▸ Are you at home during the day, or always on the road or in an office?
- ▸ Are you able to cook and enjoy cooking, or do you hate it or not have the time?
- ▸ What is the maximum amount that you're able to spend on food per month?
- ▸ How much time can you spend on preparing your meals and shopping for your food?
- ▸ Do you have time for breakfast, lunch, and dinner, and where are you normally at these times of day?
- ▸ Do you prefer sitting down for a meal or grazing on snacks throughout the day?

Of course, you can change anything you want, but in the long run, only a few can make a complete 180-degree turn in their lives when that change falls totally outside their normal lifestyle. If you want to ensure your success, don't try to follow the lifestyle of your neighbors or those in commercials. Make an effort to create **your own personal routine**. This is the only way you will be able to actually stick to those changes in the long run.

There are two more major points I want to stress. Both are of utmost importance, not only for your beauty, but also for your health.

One is **staying properly hydrated**, preferably with water or herbal tea. You need to drink enough fluids throughout the day to remain hydrated. This is critical, because in my experience, most people forget to drink enough, or they drink coffee or alcohol, which has a negative impact not only on our metabolism, but on our health and beauty. Please develop a daily routine for keeping yourself properly hydrated.

Let me give you some useful tips to help:

▶ If you find yourself forgetting to drink water, try setting reminders for yourself. If you do this for two weeks, it will help you to create a healthy habit and prevent you from forgetting again. There are many drink tracker apps available, or you can just use the alarm on your phone.

▶ Determine the minimum quantity of water you need to drink during the day, and be mindful to do this every day.

Here is a little help on how you can calculate your daily water intake:

The first step is to know your weight in pounds. The amount of water a person should drink varies on their weight. You need to calculate 67% of your weight to determine how much water to drink daily.[14] For example, if you weigh 150 pounds, you would calculate 67% and learn you should be drinking about 100 ounces of water every day (100 ounces equal 2.84 liters). Finally, you need to adjust that number based on your workouts. You should add 12 ounces of water to your daily total for every 30 minutes that you work out. So, if you work out for 60 minutes daily, you would add 24 ounces of water to your daily intake.

If you do not like water, there are so many things you can do to jazz it up. For example, you can throw in some lemon or lime wedges, mint leaves, or fruit to help give it flavor and make it delicious. There are also some organic, sugar free and healthy powders you can add to water for a more interesting flavor.

The second most important point is regarding **deprivation and starvation** as popular weight-loss methods. It's important for you to realize that when I talk about proper nutrition, I never mean starvation. Starvation is never the answer! If you understand how your body works, it will become immediately obvious why this is so. Humans, like all living organisms, are fundamentally governed by two instinctual drives: **survival** and **reproduction.** When you begin to starve yourself, your body reacts as if it has been exposed to danger and switches over to its survival function. This means that your body begins to break down your muscles, which are a great

---

14 Kristen McCaffrey, "How to calculate how much water you should drink a day," Slender Kitchen, https://www.slenderkitchen.com/article/how-to-calculate-how-much-water-you-should-drink-a-day.

source of energy, to make up for the calorie deficit.[15] Ultimately, starvation diets will slow down your metabolism. Think about when the fuel level in your car is too low and you switch off all unnecessary functions and avoid revving up your engine. Just like a car, your body switches into an energy saving mode. Then, as soon as your body has access to food again, it will immediately start storing excess fat to help your body survive. There are several good weight loss programs that will help you slim down and have a fit body, but if you select a program that requires you to deprive yourself of food or starve yourself, it will hurt your body, health and metabolism in the long run!

You'll want to consider the below formula when you create your nutrition plan:

Nutrition for an amazing physique = proper nutrition and fluid intake (healthy, balanced, consumed with regularity) + **personalization** (considering your preferences, lifestyle, individual abilities, family history/genetics and sensitivities) + **persistence.**

EXERCISE

Many people think that if they eat healthily and follow a diet carefully, they will not need to exercise at all. While you can lose weight by dieting only, it will take much more time and won't give you a toned physique. Remember: facilitating or speeding up weight loss is not the only purpose of exercising. Physical activity gives you so much more than that! Not only will it boost your mood and enhance your overall health, it will also give you a

---

15 Meredith Crilly, "Which Burns First, Fat or Muscle?" Livestrong, January 13, 2019, https://www.livestrong.com/article/471359-which-burns-first-fat-or-muscle/.

beautiful posture, a toned and shapely figure and health benefits such as an improved cardiovascular system. The many benefits of exercise for your mental and physical health cannot be overlooked.

HOW SHOULD I EXERCISE AND HOW OFTEN?

First off, it's not enough if you exercise only because you want everyone to know that you did your workout for the day. In today's society, a lot of people fall into the trap of exercising improperly, just to say they did it. They hit the gym, or go running, or do a workout at home and appear to be exercising, but they do it inappropriately. They don't make an effort or break out of their comfort zone. Those who work out at the right intensity will be the ones who see results, not those who work out only because they want to brag about it and post selfies on social media to appear trendy or fit.

Your intensity depends on your reasons for exercising. Do you want to improve your stamina, lose weight, gain muscle tone or train for a competition? A proper level of intensity depends on these goals. For weight loss, the more intense or longer your activity, the more calories you can burn.

Those who are planning well, focusing and making an effort have done everything they possibly can to make their training worthwhile. What is wonderful about training this way is that when you run into friends after two or three months, they notice your progress! Of course, balance is still important. Overdoing it can increase the risk of soreness or injury. If you are new to exercising, gradually build up the intensity and be responsible about your health. This is a lifetime commitment, not a sprint. Talk to your doctor if you have any medical conditions and ask for help from professional experts like personal trainers if you are not sure how intensely you should exercise.

And now we have arrived at the question: *how often should I exercise?*

In my experience, achieving the best result requires you to exercise for at least two or three times per week. Dedicating the time to working out three to five times a week with the above attitude and effort is even better. For your efforts to reflect on your health and appearance, I would recommend that frequency, but make sure you have enough rest too, because you can only improve if you give your body time to recover. If you do intensive workouts, you need a minimum of one to two days off per week. Of course, if you feel your body needs more rest, then listen to it. There are more intense and rigorous workout regiments, like HIIT training, but I would caution against starting out at that intensity. Take the time to build up your stamina before trying a more rigorous workout plan. Your body will thank you!

If you are having a busy week and you know that you won't be able to go to the gym or exercise at home more than once, don't even think about skipping that session. Put your maximum effort into that one workout and that will help make up for the ones that you are missing that week. You can also try working in physical exercise in other ways if you think you'll miss a workout, like parking further away in a parking lot so you have to walk more or taking the stairs instead of riding in the elevator.

The same goes for the length of time dedicated to your workouts. If you are not able to exercise for 60 minutes or more at this stage of your life, and all you can accomplish is 20–30 minutes, then do what you can at your maximum effort. I am one of the many instructors who disapprove of the notion that a workout that lasts less than 30 minutes is a waste of time. It can be effective too, especially when building up your stamina and resilience. What is important is that you need to step out of your comfort zone and do your best.

If you are unmotivated or discouraged, you may ask yourself, "What's the point?" If similar thoughts have ever crossed your mind, then I'm going to ask you to consider this carefully:

Is there a difference between someone who works out for 20 minutes, three times a week, and someone who chooses not to workout at all because they can only manage less than 30 minutes? Yes! The first person will get about 52 hours of exercise per year, which burns approximately 35,000 calories, even at medium intensity, while the latter case is at ZERO calories burned.

What will be the difference between these two people be after 5 years? 10 years? 20 years?

Everything counts, as Brian Tracy, the world-renowned author, life coach and professional public speaker would say.[16] Everything counts! Every training session you do counts.

---

16 "Everything Counts! How to Make a Good First Impression," Brian Tracy, YouTube, January 4, 2013, https://www.youtube.com/watch?v=BFSXyD-ycjY.

GUIDELINES FOR CHOOSING A PHYSICAL ACTIVITY THAT IS RIGHT FOR YOU

LOOK FOR PROFESSIONALISM!

In my experience, many instructors don't have sufficient knowledge. Many fitness coaches are not qualified. Now, what I mean by "qualified" is not only the title, certification, or credentials, but the knowledge. During my Beautyrobic sessions, I have met many guests who have always worked out regularly but still don't know the correct way to crunch. I began to wonder why no one ever called their attention to this error or taught them the correct execution of the exercise. We risk physical injury when we work out incorrectly, so how we do it can make or break us, literally!

I believe that someone who trains another physically must have a sound understanding of the basic principles and fundamentals of the body. This knowledge should include how exercise affects the body internally, how the body and muscles function, and the proper execution of each movement. Until an instructor has learned all these things, they may put someone's body and health at risk while teaching classes. In my Beautyrobic instructor course, I teach the new instructors all the knowledge they need to teach a professional Beautyrobic workout class.

LOOK AT THE RESULTS!

Every sport and exercise—cardio, yoga, weightlifting, team sports, hiking, dancing, etc.—has a different effect on our muscles, radiance, and even the way we move and carry ourselves every day, consequently producing different end results. A swimmer, rower, ballerina, bodybuilder, and a Beautyrobic woman will all have completely different physiques. A lady who goes to Beautyrobic looks and walks differently than a swimmer, rower, or bodybuilder. If you know or have ever run into a wrestler, a bodybuilder, a ballerina, or even a lady who goes to Beautyrobic on the street, then you know exactly what I'm talking about.

The movements practiced in a person's regular sport becomes ingrained in their everyday movements.

It's up to you to decide what result you wish to achieve and then choose your activity accordingly. You may also want to meet the instructor so that you can decide whether you identify with them. It helps if you like their physique or feel that you can identify with their personality. I recommend choosing a workout, sport, or activity that is interesting to you as well.

CONSIDER YOUR LIFESTYLE AND PERSONALITY!

At-home exercise routines are great, but if you pay for them and never use them, you will not make any improvements. Similarly, if you have no time to attend a group workout class or a gym because it does not fit your schedule, it will prevent you from exercising. You must take your lifestyle and schedule into account when choosing a class or exercise routine. Your lifestyle is not an obstacle to exercising, only an excuse. There is no shortage of options for you to choose from, so find the one that suits you best!

TRY IT OUT TO SEE IF YOU ENJOY IT!

One of my favorite sayings is, *workout because you love your body, not because you hate it.*

Don't exercise because it's a duty, but because you enjoy it!

The secret is to find a type of exercise that suits your body and that you love so much that you incorporate it into your life *on a regular basis.* You have to be excited about doing it. There are so many types of exercise you can choose from, and the reason some people don't exercise consistently is because they don't listen to their feelings. They choose a type of exercise they don't enjoy and then put off doing it. However, with exercise, the whole point is to do it consistently to produce lasting results.

I can't tell you how many times I've heard from women at Beautyrobic classes that all types of exercise they have done did not work so they abandoned them. They are happy to have found Beautyrobic because they finally found an exercise program they really love and can stick to. Believe me, something you don't love is unsustainable in the long run. So, keep trying various forms of exercise until you find the one that makes you feel amazing. Then you are on the right path!

You can apply the previous nutrition formula to exercise too:

Exercise for an amazing physique = Proper Workout (Professional, Effective, and suits your goals) **+ Personalization** (considering your lifestyle, interests, and individual abilities) **+ Persistence and Consistency**

MOVEMENT

There is a famous story about Marilyn Monroe that illustrates how a woman's movements affect how seductive she is.[17] Marilyn Monroe was a famous movie star, swarmed by a crowd of fans wherever she went. One day, she was in the Grand Central Station in New York with a journalist and a photographer. She wanted to show the two men that it was a matter of choice whether her fans saw her as the celebrated film star or the ordinary Norma Jean Baker, her birth name. The men were surprised to find that no one recognized her or even turned their head to stare at the movie star.

When she left the subway station, she suddenly transformed into the celebrated movie star. She fluffed her hair and began to walk and move like the movie star version of herself. Suddenly people began to recognize her and were stopping to watch her. Within no time, she was surrounded by a huge mob of fans.[18] You wouldn't believe how much power lies with a woman who is graceful and feminine in her motions.

This will become second nature to you with practice. No one is born a femme fatale, but with enough practice and perseverance, you can become whoever you want! And since you usually train not once, but repeatedly, the movements you practice become built in.

---

17 Olivia Fox Cabane, *The Charisma Myth: How Anyone Can Master the Art and Science of Personal Magnetism* (New York: Penguin, 2013): 1.
18 Ibid.

If you want to become more feminine and attractive, do a workout that isolates graceful movements, makes you more feminine and improves your posture. The goal is to integrate your gracefulness, flexibility, and femininity into exercise. If you're currently doing a workout that doesn't include this, choose one that offers this as an add-on—something that's feminine and makes your movements softer and more graceful, like Beautyrobic workouts, which are specifically tailored to women's bodies and contains lot of feminine movements. Other good examples are ballet, Pilates, yoga, or Latin dance.

POSTURE

Time and time again, I see women who are genetically slim, have a sedentary lifestyle, or are just busy with work and don't find it essential to incorporate regular exercise into their lives. The result is poor posture and poor quality of movement that will only get worse with time. Good posture and proper activation of your core muscles is more important than you might think. It is not only important for your health, but beautiful posture makes people elegant and regal.

WHAT CAN YOU DO TO ACHIEVE BEAUTIFUL POSTURE?

Pay attention to your sitting position at your job and at home. If you do an Internet search on the correct way to sit in a chair, you will see plenty of videos and articles showing you proper ergonomics and the best chair for your posture. You can even get an exercise ball to use as a chair! When I worked in an office, I had an exercise ball and a chair, and I used them interchangeably.

Exercise regularly, and if possible, choose an exercise program that targets the core muscles around your abdomen as the primary focus. At Beautyrobic, we place critical importance on strengthening the core muscles, and for good reason! A professional instructor is aware of the importance of exercising the core muscles on a regular basis.

Something you may not pay attention to is your bed! You spend several hours sleeping on your mattress and pillows. Choosing the wrong mattress or pillows can negatively impact your quality of sleep and/or posture over time. Luckily nowadays there are many choices based on your needs. Examples include your height, health issues and personal preferences like sleeping positions. So, make sure you choose the best one that fits you the most and support your health.

FLEXIBILITY

Many people would not think so, but flexibility greatly affects the quality of both your posture and your gait. Regular stretching increases your range of motion and keeps you flexible, giving you a graceful and youthful look. I always tell my guests that if they want to stay youthful as long as possible, they should pay close attention to maintaining their resilience both in body and in spirit as the years go by. If people paid attention to maintaining their flexibility in body and mind, they would look more youthful.

As the body ages, the skin becomes less elastic, muscles become more rigid, and tendons get stiffer. These all add to the appearance of aging, along with weakness and difficulty moving and bending. Maintaining flexibility reduces these effects for a more youthful physical appearance and better mobility.[19] It's amazing to see gymnasts in their 70s or 80s who seem at least 10–20 years younger than their contemporaries. So, regular stretching not only promotes beautiful posture and elegant walking, but also helps preserve our youth for a long time. This is why our Beautyrobic Sense class is aimed at stretching expressively and, thanks to the special atmosphere and body caresses, it even unleashes your sensuality.

Try our Beautyrobic, Beautyrobic Core, and Beautyrobic Sense workout programs that not only effectively tone and burn fat, but also help improve your posture, boost your self-confidence, and enhance your femininity! All three workouts have been designed for women, therefore they are geared toward the anatomical characteristics of women.

CLOTHING AND STYLE

Dressing well matters a great deal, since a flattering outfit can cover up your flaws and draw attention to your best assets, but a less-than-fortunate one can highlight your problem areas. When I talk about clothing, style, and dressing your best, the first thing that comes to my mind is the following saying:

---

19 "Why Flexibility is So Significant As We Age," Unique Health and Fitness, April 27, 2019, https://www.uniquehealthandfitness.com/why-flexibility-is-so-significant-as-we-age.

Dress for the job you want, not the job you have!

It also makes me think of two stories. The first happened to me personally. Before I ran my own business, I worked at a printing company as a team leader in the IT department. My boss and everyone in the office dressed how you might expect someone in IT to dress. My boss did not put too much emphasis on suits. He would wear simple T-shirts with jeans. I was the opposite. I loved dressing in a feminine but businesslike manner, wearing blazers, pencil skirts, and elegant pumps. I remember one particular instance when I was having a conversation with a colleague from another department, and he was taken aback when he realized I wasn't the boss. Up until that very moment, he had assumed I was the boss. It was clear to me there was only one explanation and that was how I was dressed. The reason he believed I was the head of the department is because I always dressed like I was, whereas the people around me dressed more casually.

The other story I want to share with you is an experience one of my colleagues had. He used to visit our company frequently because he was one of our suppliers. When I first met him, he was a salesperson, but he always dressed as if he was the CEO. Now, he is the deputy CEO of the company. It would be too much to say that this is due his style alone, but I am 100% convinced that it played an important role in his successive promotions and in shaping his career as a whole. This points to the importance of fashion and how relevant it is to you as a person.

"What a strange power there is in clothing."

—Isaac Bashevis Singer[20]

Nobel Prize-winning author Isaac Bashevis Singer asserts that the clothes we wear hold considerable power.[21] In line with this assertion, bestselling books such *as Dress for Success* by John T. Molloy and TV shows like TLC's *What Not to Wear* emphasize the power that clothes can have over others by creating favorable (or otherwise) impressions. Indeed, a host of research has documented the effects that people's clothes have on the perceptions of others. And the clothes we wear have power not only over others, but also over ourselves.[22]

Remember to ask yourself the questions:

*Who am I really? What is the message that
I wish to convey about myself?*

How you dress is one of the most important messages you can send about yourself.

Of course, I know many highly successful people who would never wear a suit and tie and are still heavy hitters in their profession (especially in the IT sector, startups, or entrepreneurship), so

---

20 Charles Spence, *Sensehacking: How to Use the Power of Your Senses for Happier, Healthier Living* (London: Penguin, 2021): 215.

21 Ibid.

22 Hajo Adam and Adam D. Galinsky, "Enclothed Cognition," *Journal of Experimental Social Psychology* (2012): 1, https://www.doi.org/10.1016/j.jesp.2012.02.008.

fashion is not the only important factor. However, how you dress will strongly influence other people's perception of you and will form their first impression. So, try to be credible in your dress because it projects an impression about where you belong in society. How you dress may also be a decisive factor when it comes to choosing a partner. I have a dear friend who is a successful lawyer, and always looks impeccable and perfectly polished. When I spoke to him about attractiveness and the qualities he looks for in an ideal partner, a stylish appearance played a part. He didn't say it was the single most important characteristic to look for in a woman, but it *does* matter!

A nicely put-together outfit can accentuate your beauty and best features while concealing your flaws. As is true with makeup and hair, it is even more relevant that you should never follow fashion trends blindly, but instead find what flatters you personally. Your dress should be appropriate for the situations you find yourself in regularly and be in perfect harmony with your personality. In other words, it is very important that you find your own personal style and express your self-confidence! If you find your personal style, that will be half the battle won in Level 1.

Most people don't ask help from a professional stylist because they think it will be too expensive. But as I see it, it costs much more to spend your money on unflattering clothes, versus consulting a professional about what is genuinely flattering for you! Every body shape—short, tall, slim, athletic, hourglass, curvy, etc.—is complemented by different fashion styles and the way clothes hang off the body. Clothing colors and accents can also enhance natural beauty traits like your hair and skin tone. Your lifestyle, career, and personality should also be reflected in your clothing style to attract people to you that have similar interests and tastes.

Five tips about fashion every woman should know:

1. When looking for a style that is your own, you may seek inspiration from the world of haute couture, fashion magazines and the Internet. My advice is not to recreate those styles, but to use them as inspiration, so you can add some excitement and uniqueness to your outfits.

2. Most celebrities are dressed by professional stylists, so you usually can't go wrong if you draw inspiration from their wardrobe and fashion sense, especially those known for their sophisticated style.

3. When it comes to clothing and seduction, often less is more. In other words, if we want potential partners to take us seriously, we should refrain from clothes that put every part of our body on display. Doing this can make you look like your goal is casual sex, which is fine if that *is* your goal, but sends the wrong message if it isn't. Everyone desires what is hard to get. If you choose the right clothes, you can reveal some of your amazing physique without being overly revealing. Instead, choose accessories or use tricks that stimulate the imagination of the opposite sex and excite their attention. The secret is in the (sexy) details.

4. I believe that even things that are invisible to the eyes of others can work miracles on your allure. Let me explain what I mean by that. If you are wearing incredibly sexy red lingerie under your dress, that will have a strong effect

on you and your confidence. Because *you* know about it and that will have an influence on your magnetism.

5. Always keep yourself neat, well-groomed and well-dressed, even if you live alone. Doing so will help it become a habit. You must never, ever neglect yourself. Make sure that you are always fresh, clean and well-groomed. Do this for yourself!

For more information about styling, you will find my interview with professional stylist at the link below:

www.mindfulmagneticwoman.com/gift

So, I hope it's now clear that having a put-together appearance doesn't depend on the characteristics you were born with, but on working to improve what you have. For a complete makeover, all it takes is to break it up into smaller tasks and tackle them one by one. If you cannot find time to browse the Internet or seek inspiration from magazines, the best thing you can do is to rely on professionals, since they have dedicated years to becoming top-notch experts in their fields. Think of it as an investment in yourself.

Invest in the most important thing: yourself!

Once you have decided to hire a professional, make sure you put yourself in the hands of a real professional!

To help you with this, I'd like to give you a guide on **how to find the best expert.**

GO THROUGH THE BELOW CHECKLIST AND YOU CAN'T GO WRONG!

▶ **Look at their work.** You don't need to be a detective to look up a person on the Internet. Use all the advantages offered by social media profiles and business pages and do your research. You can find information through an Internet search, but don't forget to ask your friends for their opinions too.

▶ **Do you identify with them?** Someone may be an expert in their profession, but if their body of work doesn't match your taste, then this expert is not the person you are looking for.

▶ **What do people say about them?** Professional expertise is one thing, but how do they treat people? How conscientious are they? Do they listen and do what's best for their clients?

▶ **Ask for an appointment or a consultation.** When you meet in person or virtually, there will always be an energy exchange of some sort. If you are not on the same wavelength or they didn't leave you with a positive impression or even irritated you, they are definitely not the person you are looking for. Rely on your intuition, and don't start working with them until you have made sure that the two of you have a chemistry that is a good match for working together successfully!

SO, WHAT DO YOU DO WHEN YOU FEEL YOU HAVE FOUND THE *ONE*, THE BEAUTY EXPERT WHO IS JUST *PERFECT* FOR YOU?

The two of you should talk! You need to tell them what you wish to achieve.

Don't forget to ask yourself:

Who am I really? What is the message I wish to convey about myself?

Don't limit this to expressing yourself in words alone, but also in photos or videos. Let me clarify why that matters… Let's say you tell your stylist that you want a revolutionary, innovative business wardrobe. Will "revolutionary" mean the exact same thing to them as to you? Perhaps what is too conservative for them is very revolutionary for you, or vice versa. So, it is important to remember that it's not enough to explain your wishes verbally, you must also make sure that the two of you are on the same page visually. Often, miscommunication is the main source of dissatisfaction.

AND NOW, THE CONCLUSION OF LEVEL 1

I wish to reiterate something very important to make sure it is clear. This chapter deals with appearance—with the outward, physical features—which does indeed matter, as I have substantiated with proof, whether you want to recognize this or not. The reason this is at the first level is because this is the first and most basic level of being attractive and magnetic. When you meet someone for the first time, the first thing you perceive is their appearance. If you do not take care of yourself at this level, you will have a very tough time later on. As the saying goes: *you never get a second chance to make a good first impression.* This level is not about requiring you to be young, beautiful and perfect, which I hope has become obvious. What it does require you to do is to take care of your appearance, pay attention to your body, and care about how you look. If you dedicate some time to this and take my advice, you will create an appearance that harmonizes with your personality, style and lifestyle, and makes you feel good about yourself. This is my goal with this level.

Successful businesses work in a way that, although the company may not be perfect in everything (nobody and nothing can be perfect in everything), there are one or two things in the company that truly stand out. In all the other areas, it has to meet a certain standard. If there is one thing that falls below the standard, that one thing may bring the whole company down.

Imagine a company that produces fantastic products and has a great website but has below-par customer service in terms of manners or reliability. You may not care how great the products are and go elsewhere because of the customer service. The same applies when considering our own personal success and attractiveness. Even if you are not a beauty queen, if you have a great sense of humor or an above-average IQ, people will adore you! But if you have a great sense of humor or an above-average IQ, and your appearance is unacceptable, that will seriously undermine your chances for success overall. You could be passed over for a less intelligent but average looking woman. Of course, the opposite is also true! If someone is exceptionally beautiful, but she is dumb as a post, rude or has negative energy, men will substitute her for a less-beautiful but nicer woman.

This is why I'm asking you to get down to it and do the work at each and every level of your attractiveness, from the first level to the upper levels. No matter how exceptional you may be at something, if there is something else in which you are below standard, that one thing will seriously undermine your chances for success and happiness. It is my goal for you not simply to become physically attractive, but to **unlock your inner and outer glow and maximize your Real Attractiveness.**

chapter three

LEVEL II: K.O.

KNOCK 'EM OUT...

From the moment I decided to write this book, every man who crossed my path could count on me asking them one very specific question: *What makes a woman particularly attractive to you?* I also asked men on social media, at conferences and practically everywhere I went. Theories written in books are one thing, but how actual real-life men view attractiveness is another.

At times, I would phrase my question this way: *Suppose there are beautiful, identical twin sisters. What criteria would you use to choose one over the other?* Before hearing their responses, I assumed they would choose the more intelligent woman. Well, their responses surprised me. Although men *do* value intelligence, this wasn't the primary factor for them! Men said they would choose the kinder and more thoughtful sister. Kindness was the most important trait for almost all the men I asked. In fact, often when they complained about their previous relationships, one of the main reasons for the breakup was a lack of kindness. What is so surprising about this is not that kindness and thoughtfulness matters, but rather its level of importance.

One of the best examples of this I've seen was a video I saw online that perfectly illustrated the power of true, heartfelt kindness. Kindness and love have incredible power, and if used well, they can conquer the world. In the video, a father and his little boy and little girl are playing a game. The point of the game was that the father would clasp his hands and ask the kids to open his interlaced fingers. The little boy used all his strength and tried to pull his father's fingers apart by force, but this was in vain, of course, because the father was much stronger. Then came the little girl, who did not try to force anything, but went over and hugged her father, who could not resist her. She melted his heart, and the father immediately opened his arms and hugged his little girl back. I think it tells us everything about how powerful kindness and gentleness is.

The name of this level comes from two words: "K" for Kindness and "O" for Openness. The abbreviation is K.O. for a very specific reason. If you learn this technique in the game of magnetism, you will win by a knockout. This is why it is so crucial that you master this level!

I know plenty of intelligent women who are beautiful and have a great job and a solid financial background, but still can't find their perfect match. In fact, I have to say that many of these women tend to be on the more distant, aloof side and they are not necessarily considered kind. No matter how intelligent they are, if they are perceived as an ice queen, superior or overly tough, they may be considered unkind.

In contrast, what about women who are considered pretty, pay attention to their looks (Level 1), and are also kind, decent and thoughtful… but are, say, not so brainy? They often find love and lead a happy life beside a successful man who fits the bill in every respect. I have heard women complain about this many times, but now, after completing my research, it is perfectly clear why things work this way.

I must be very clear that I'm not saying that intelligence doesn't count. Remember, we are only on Level 2 and the higher levels are yet to come. What I'm positive about is that if a woman's intelligence is coupled with an insufferable demeanor, it does not matter how good she looks or how intelligent she is because most guys will run from her. He will choose another partner who may be less physically attractive or less brilliant but shows him kindness and warmth.

It is true that EQ, the emotional intelligence quotient, is much more important than IQ. How you treat others, how good you are at establishing and maintaining interpersonal bonds, how well and to what extent you can perceive the emotional state of the person you are communicating with, how empathetic you are toward others… all these factors determine your EQ and play a dominant role when it comes to your appeal.

I had a lengthy conversation with a good friend of mine. He is a successful businessman and a member of the board of the Hungarian Bodybuilding and Fitness Association and the International

Federation of Bodybuilding and Fitness (IFBB), as well as the founder of the biggest fitness trade show in Hungary. Due to the nature of his job, he is constantly surrounded by gorgeous-looking women, so a striking appearance alone is not enough to spark his interest. I asked him to tell me: what would make a woman stand out from the crowd in his eyes? He responded that it takes genuine, natural kindness, tolerance and a positive attitude for a woman to be able to rouse his curiosity. Mutual respect is an indispensable cornerstone of a healthy relationship for him.

Remember: attraction between two people always derives from the type of relationship they have. If you oppress, disrespect or treat the other person coldly, they will feel uncomfortable around you and won't be attracted to you. On the other hand, if a person enjoys your company, feels energized in your presence and happy, they will want to be around you as often as possible. This is because **people will always want to be around those who make them feel good, lift their spirits and energize, nurture and revive them!** No one wants to be around negative people who bring their mood down, and drain and depress them!

Olivia Fox Cabane, a prominent researcher on the topic of charisma, attributed two of her well-known charisma types to this very level. One of which is called the Kindness Charisma.[23] The Kindness Charisma is best exhibited by the Dalai Lama or Princess Diana, who were beloved by people from many countries all over the world. Kindness doesn't mean constantly faking a big smile or being overly nice. It does not involve loudly expressing your excitement all the time, being over the top or being omnipresent in someone's life. It's not about constantly doing things for others,

---

23 Cabane, *The Charisma Myth*, 71.

being a people pleaser or saying yes to every request you receive. Kindness is none of these things!

So, what is it?

?

"K" FOR KINDNESS

To manifest genuine, radiant kindness, you will need the following things:

1. Be kind to yourself.
    Be in an intimate relationship with yourself (outside and inside).

2. Be kind to others.
    Exhibit compassion, selflessness, and empathy toward others.

BE KIND TO YOURSELF!

Radiating genuine, sincere kindness is hard if you detest yourself and your life. How can you radiate kindness when you're constantly unhappy and hate yourself inside? If this describes you, you won't be able to show genuine kindness, even if you try. It will come off as forced and fake. When something is not genuine, others can sense it and their reaction will not be the one you were seeking. Remember: people sense non-verbal signs more than verbal words,[24] so, even if you try to say something nice, people will sense that you feel imbalanced inside and it will negatively affect their perception of your charisma. It is extremely important that you truly love yourself, or at the very least, accept yourself and your life!

Learn to treat yourself kindly! Many of us are constantly beating ourselves up, comparing ourselves to others, judging, berating and reprimanding ourselves. We always seek to measure up to the expectations of everyone else: society, friends, acquaintances or strangers on the Internet. The only thing we aren't tending to are our own needs. Stop punishing yourself and learn to accept that you are only human; you cannot be perfect all the time!

Nor do you need to be perfect for others to accept you. Use your best judgment, and if you make a mistake, then do your best to correct it. Do yourself this favor. You can relieve so many anxious, nervous thoughts and feelings by quieting the self-criticism and negativity inside your head. You will experience greater life satisfaction and notice improvements in your relationships and social skills. Furthermore, it may even be beneficial for your health and immune function.

The Mayo Clinic discusses the benefits of positive thinking and how to change negative thought patterns into positive thought patterns.[25] Positive thinking reduces distress, lowers the risk of depression, creates better psychological and physical well-being, and increases coping skills in times of hardship and stress.[26]

---

24 "How Much of Communication Is Nonverbal?" The University of Texas Permian Basin, accessed June 7, 2022, https://online.utpb.edu/about-us/articles/communication/how-much-of-communication-is-nonverbal/.

25 "Positive Thinking: Stop Negative Self-Talk to Reduce Stress," Mayo Clinic, January 21, 2020, https://www.mayoclinic.org/healthy-lifestyle/stress-management/in-depth/positive-thinking/art-20043950.

26 Ibid.

To put positive thinking into practice, you have to put a different spin on negative thoughts. Instead of thinking, "I've never done that before," think, "This is a great opportunity." Instead of thinking, "This is too difficult," think, "I'll tackle it from a different angle." When you think about how you feel about yourself, rather than thinking, "I'm not very pretty," think, "I love my smile (or another physical feature)."

If you feel dissatisfied with yourself, your life or your circumstances, instead of being hard on yourself, *change* something! If there's something that you find truly dissatisfying, it's up to you to do something about it. Make those changes with the utmost respect and love for yourself in mind.

There will always be situations or circumstances that are beyond your total control. Even in these cases, berating yourself will never solve anything. You need to change your perspective. Look for and focus on the positive aspects of the situation.

There are so many people to look at as an example. I always think of Nick Vujicic. He was born without hands and legs, but despite all the adversity he had to endure, he was able to overcome his circumstances and lead a happy, healthy, confident life. Instead of wallowing in self-pity, he found his life purpose by adding value to the world through motivational speaking and helping others find their own happiness in the face of adversity.[27]

There is no excuse! The longest and most intimate relationship you will ever have is with yourself. You must treat the most important person in your life with kindness. That person is **YOU!**

Important notice: If you really feel you cannot handle

---

27 Peter Bowes, "The man who leads with no limbs," BBC, March 18, 2015, https://www.bbc.com/worklife/article/20150318-leading-without-limbs.

your negative thoughts alone or you suffer from depression or anxiety, it is crucial to ask for professional help. Mental health is serious and requires help from experts.

To be able to truly love yourself and your life, you must learn to appreciate what you already have, and feel grateful for it.

Gratitude is an important philosophy practiced in many meditations intended to increase positivity.[28] Whether it is for something tangible—the roof over your head, your children, the food on your table—or something intangible, like the love of a spouse or partner, gratitude can decrease the risk of depression, increase immune function and provide a positive and uplifting outlook on your life and yourself.

Be grateful for who you are and for all the good things in your life. Think of even the smallest things, the simple ones that perhaps you take for granted. These little things could mean the world to someone else.

Please do the following exercise:

EXERCISE

Write down the things you are grateful for.

---

28 "Gratitude Meditation," Headspace, https://www.headspace.com/meditation/gratitude.

Do this practice every day for a month. After the first month, do it at least once a week going forward.

Make a list of everything you have to be grateful for! What are the things you are thankful for in yourself, your body, your life, or your surroundings?

This exercise will work wonders to help you recognize all the blessings that surround you. What you have right now can fill your heart with joy and gratitude if you learn to be mindful and treat those blessings with focused attention. This will fill you with positive energy and gratitude every day of your life.

BE KIND TO OTHERS!

There's another very important component to kindness: extending compassion, selflessness and empathy towards the people around you. Make an effort to never be spiteful or focus on the negative attributes in others, even if they do things you don't approve of.

I had a friend who I thought was a kind, humble woman until I did something she didn't like. Then, suddenly, aggressive and judgmental traits came out of her. I didn't even recognize her. I was stunned. Everything she had built up about herself—this kind, positive, attractive image—was destroyed in a moment. Of course, I saw right away that this was more about making up for her own insecurities and fear of losing. So, I intentionally didn't retaliate. I didn't put gas on the fire by trying to win but calmed her down and discussed it. But from then on, I didn't want to be in her company and we didn't get along the same way we used to, and you can be sure that I wasn't the only one who noticed this behavior. Before you attack anyone for anything, stop and realize that we're all people and can communicate to work things out.

Most of the time, it's just a misunderstanding that can be discussed. However, it may happen that someone is terribly mean and catty to you for no reason. I have developed a good tactic to handle it! I have made a habit of trying to understand the perspective of the other person and the reason why they might have acted the way they did. There are situations where, despite all my efforts, I just can't find a reasonable explanation for that person's actions. Even then, I focus on what that person must have gone through in their life that led them to be the way they are. It is important to recognize that when someone is being rude, angry or judgmental, it is more of a reflection of their life and personal feelings than a reflection of who you are. This helps take away any anger or frustration. Instead, I tend to feel sorry for them because they must have had to endure hardships in their life to make them that way. I don't let their circumstances bring me down, but I do show empathy and compassion for what they've gone through.

You should always stop and try to look at things from the other person's point of view. Of course, that's easier said than done when someone angers you. If you choose to get upset about the behavior of others, you won't cause pain to *them*, you will only hurt *yourself*. Do yourself a favor, or rather a kindness, and refuse to hate. Be kind and learn to smile at the world! Praise and compliment others often! Be generous with words of encouragement. You have no idea how much joy you can bring to the world by doing this.

REMOVE YOURSELF FROM NEGATIVE ENVIRONMENTS!

Speaking of kindness, I have a good piece of advice for you. If you find yourself in a situation where people are criticizing someone else behind their back, negatively gossiping or having arguments, try to keep yourself out of the fray. Let me explain why this is important.

Such discussions do nothing to improve your attractiveness and charisma in the eyes of others. When it comes to gossip, whether you are right or wrong, whether the debate itself is pointless or meaningful, the consequences could be devastating. Most people feel uncomfortable in negative environments and, sooner or later, they will try to avoid them.

Secondly, if you do get into an argument, you will never truly emerge as a winner. If your position is wrong and you lose an argument, you will find yourself in an unpleasant situation, having been defeated. If your position is right and you win the argument, that could also be awkward as it could be a distressing experience for those defeated. In the future, they may avoid you, because no one wants to be the loser in their social group.

Take this to heart: A wise woman will never force her truth on another, even if she is right. Instead, she will live her truth, planting seeds, subtly arranging things so that in the end she will imperceptivity have her way, and everything will be how she imagined!

Consider this: which is stronger, the wind or the sun? If a storm rages with hurricane-force winds, it won't be able to blow your coat off. The harder the wind blows, the more closely you will wrap your coat around you. The sun, however, will shine on you, surrounding you with warmth, until you take your coat off by choice.

Imagine kindness in a similar way!

The more pressure you put on someone to adopt your ideas and opinions, the faster that person will shut the door on you. However, if you make an effort to understand their point of view, slowly and patiently aligning it with your own, you may find that they will accept your position of their own free will.

I used this same approach with my husband last spring when I felt exhausted and needed a vacation. I picked an amazing trip to the Canary Islands and suggested to him that we book it and take a break. But he was bursting with energy and enthusiasm for his work and didn't feel like leaving. No matter how hard I pushed, I just couldn't talk him into it. I tried nagging him and even throwing a tantrum, but to no avail. He said it was not the right time because he had too much to do. So, I changed my strategy. I stopped being pushy, difficult and trying to bulldoze him. Instead, I talked to him sincerely about how tired and listless I was feeling and how much I needed to recharge. This strategy worked, and we went on vacation for a week! In the end, he said he loved the trip and admitted that it was a marvelous idea.

THE POWER OF A SMILE

A smile can be a very powerful thing. I'm not talking about idiotic giggling or insane grinning, but a warm smile that is filled with cheerfulness and reflects a happy, balanced inner self. Your smile reflects to others that you feel good and are willing to radiate your happiness to others.

There's nothing worse than a negative, angry person. So, be positive and smile more! Positive people tend to smile, whereas negative people complain. Be honest, would you want to wake up every morning next to a negative or bitter person for the rest of your life?

A smile is so simple and yet, so effective!

There's a song by Nat King Cole, "When You're Smiling," in which he sings, "The whole world smiles with you!"

I conducted a small experiment to prove how effective a smile is. I repeated my process several times, and it worked every single one of them! I'd like to encourage you to try it and see how it works for you.

When I was single and went out to parties with my girlfriends, there would be some occasions I was open to meeting someone new and others when I simply didn't want to be approached. When I was open to meeting people, the only thing I changed about my normal behavior was to smile. Especially at any men I wanted to connect with. In contrast, on occasions where I did not want to be approached by anyone new, I didn't smile or make eye contact with anyone. I concentrated on having a good time with my girlfriends and would not signal in any way that I was open to being approached. It brought about the desired result every time. When I was cold and standoffish, I was avoided like the plague.

So, try to be truly compassionate and kind towards others and with yourself. Then, you will wear a genuine, radiant smile. This kind of smile is not fake or stiff but says it all! There are few things sexier in the world than a genuine smile.

"O" FOR OPENNESS

The second part of this level is openness! Let me explain what type of openness I'm referring to, so we are on the same page.

When I speak of openness, I'm not referring to you completely letting your guard down, being "easy," or immediately revealing everything about yourself to someone. Doing those things may even result in someone becoming quickly bored with you, since you are no longer intriguing or challenging.

What I mean by openness is that you adopt an open and attentive attitude towards other people. Don't close yourself off and shut down in a social situation. Kindly approach people at an event and initiate a conversation. If someone approaches you, be kind and friendly. Respond to questions you are asked and engage in the conversation by asking questions. Completely avoid being negative. Be open to the other person, their thoughts and ideas, and devote attention to them.

There are people who only care about themselves and nothing else in a conversation. They have little to no regard for other people or their ideas and are completely self-absorbed. Such people are almost incapable of talking about anything other than themselves. This trait is understandably not appealing to other people. Usually after a few minutes, people will look for an opportunity to escape the conversation. In contrast, when you open up to others, express genuine interest in getting to know them, and pay attention to their responses, other people will want the pleasure of your company.

MASTER THE ART OF LISTENING!

When someone is talking to you and your mind starts wandering, the chances are that they will notice that you've tuned out—especially if you begin to stare into space with glazed eyes or are constantly averting your gaze while they are still talking to you. Humans naturally perceive non-verbal signals with a much greater intensity than verbal ones.[29] Non-verbal communication tends to convey a much stronger message, since it is the oldest form of human communication. For this very reason, even if your conversational partner has never specifically learned to read body language, they will perceive if you are unenthusiastic about what they are talking about.

When you learn to devote your undivided attention to someone during a conversation, they will continue to seek out your company in the future. You can achieve this by calling someone by their name, asking them questions, asking them about topics that interest them, paying careful attention to their replies, treating them with heartfelt consideration and keeping the conversation flowing. This will also work wonders on dates or at business functions.

Dale Carnegie said it best:

"Talk to people about themselves and they'll listen for hours."[30]

---

29 Raymond H. Hull, "The Art of Nonverbal Communication in Practice," *The Hearing Journal* 69, no. 5 (May 2016): 22, https://doi.org/10.1097/01.HJ.0000483270.59643.cc.

30 Dale Carnegie, *How to Win Friends & Influence People* (New York: Pocket Books, 1998), 83.

EXERCISE

LOOK OTHERS IN THE EYE!

If you want to be charismatic, look someone in the eye when speaking to them and nod your head in agreement when you agree with the point they are making. Nodding occasionally will show that you are paying attention to them and the conversation. Be careful not to nod continually, because you may come off as overly eager to please rather than engaged and charismatic. Provide verbal confirmations that you are listening or understanding at the appropriate intervals.

PRACTICE FOCUSED ATTENTION

If you have ever meditated, you will understand why these next exercises are so highly effective. Just as with meditation, they may be hard at first, but with practice they can be perfected by focusing your attention.

Turn your attention to one object and quiet everything else in your mind. Focus only on that one object for one minute (as you progress, you can increase the amount of time gradually). Try this same technique but now turn your focus only to your breathing or listening to your surroundings while your eyes are closed. The goal of this exercise is to increase your ability to concentrate solely on the selected object.

When someone is speaking to you, your task is to concentrate on that person and on what they are telling you, as well as on their emotions and body language. If your thoughts wander, focus on your breathing for three seconds then return your attention to the conversation!

I realize that it might seem odd that I'm discussing your magnetism but giving you a task to pay attention to other people. However, if you are attentive to others, they will be drawn to you. When people are naturally drawn to you, you will have the ability to influence them. You approached *them*, you talked about *them* and you are interested in *them*. If you invest the time and attention in a person, they may not know why, but you will linger in their minds, and they will seek out your company again. This is true for social interactions as well as professional interactions like work meetings or company functions. You want to leave people with positive memories of you, because that will present greater opportunities when you cross paths again.

Trust the process, open yourself up to other people, and give them your attention! Listen to them and be sincere and kind. I know it can be intimidating at first, especially if you are an introverted person, but it's at least worth trying. Begin opening yourself up to people and observe their reactions. If they begin to converse with you or ask questions, try to "tune in" to that person and see what happens!

A TIP TO MAKE YOU MORE LIKEABLE

A few years ago, I attended well-known life and business coach Tony Robbins' Unleash the Power Within (UPW) seminar in London, where he talked a lot about how deciding something will give you the ability to make it happen. It was a life changing experience for me. I even walked barefoot across a bed of red, hot coals that were between 1,200- and 2,000-degrees Fahrenheit! Talk about mind over matter!

At this seminar, Tony Robbins spoke at length about Neuro-Linguistic Programming[31] and how effective it is.[32] This subject sparked my interest, so I set out to learn more about it. I found and took a course to learn more about this technique and now I would like to share one of my favorite NLP techniques with you. It is called mirroring.

If you want someone to feel drawn to you, try to synchronize yourself with that person by subtly imitating their behavior and mannerisms. If they raise or lower the tone of their voice, do the same. If they lean forward, adopt a matching posture. By doing this, you will be able to resonate imperceptibly with the other person. When you manage to do this successfully, a person will open up to you and become much more receptive to your thoughts and ideas. Naturally, you must do this discreetly, because if you start mimicking them in an abnormal way it will come off as fake and that's a recipe for disaster!

THE RIGHT QUESTION

How exactly are you supposed to initiate a conversation with a stranger out of nowhere? Often when I suggest someone approach a person they

---

31 Neuro-Linguistic Programming (NLP) is the study of excellent communication, and it is often described as a user manual for your conscious and unconscious mind. It was developed by modeling effective communicators and therapists who achieved results with their clients.

32 Tony Robbins, "Neuro-Linguistic Programming Techniques: How You Can Transform Your Life with These 5 Powerful Methods," Tony Robbins, accessed June 7, 2022, https://www.tonyrobbins.com/leadership-impact/nlp-techniques/.

want to start a conversation with, they ask me, "What should I ask?" Questions should always have a purpose. If you ask about the temperature, your goal is to know what the weather is like in that moment. If you ask what time a presentation will start, your goal is to get information about the starting time. What's your goal in starting that conversation?

Is your goal to open a line of communication between you and the other person, or to have the other person like you and to enjoy your company? In that case, I suggest you don't start by asking them about the weather, because that will not get you very far! Don't ask commonplace or small talk questions. Instead, try to ask a question that intrigues the other person and evokes positive emotions. Obviously, this will differ depending on the situation and on the person, but if you do so thoughtfully, you can grab the other person's attention quickly and be on the right track. Once I was in a business event where the special guest spoke about a famous motivational speaker and one of his books in his speech. I wanted to make a connection with him, so after his speech, I brought up the book and author he mentioned in his speech, as I was reading it too. I recommended other good books and asked him if he can suggest some to me. Of course, he was really happy to share these books with me and asked me to connect on LinkedIn too. This is how I could get a good connection because of the right questions.

AND NOW,
THE CONCLUSION OF LEVEL 2

This level of my book and its takeaways are comparable to some of the best marketing techniques, in that they seem simple and obvious, yet somehow we still fail to put them into practice. I urge you not to dismiss these ideas simply because you feel like you already know them. Truly analyze and consider whether you are putting everything into practice.

Be kind. It's so simple and obvious, yet when it comes to practical application, somehow, we often fall short.

Open up to people and give them your attention. In today's world, people are becoming increasingly closed off. We have reached a point where we almost exclusively communicate on social media. Yet, when we encounter the people whose photos we are liking or commenting on in real life, we pretend we don't know them or don't see them.

IMPORTANT: Everything in this chapter should be put into practice! Practice everything intentionally and consistently!

There's a huge difference between knowing something in theory and applying it in your life. As Morpheus said in the film

The Matrix, "There is a difference between knowing the path and walking the path."[33] I urge you to go back and complete the exercises if you haven't already. If you put everything into practice in your daily life, this level will produce solid results. **Remember to be kind to others, smile and open up to other people! I know that you will be pleasantly surprised by the change that this will have on your life.**

33 The Wachowskis, dir., *The Matrix*, Warner Bros., 1999.

chapter four

LEVEL III: SELF-CONFIDENCE

SHINE FROM WITHIN

People frequently correlate attractiveness and self-confidence. If you believe in yourself and are convinced that you can attain your goals, are not intimidated by challenges but face them fearlessly, you will have an air of magnetism that's truly appealing to other people. Self-confidence is very alluring indeed.

WHY IS THAT SO?

People are often insecure about their lives and decisions. This insecurity leaves people open to being influenced by others. When someone is confident in themselves, they give others the impression that they have all the answers. Insecure people follow confident people. Confidence gives people the air of being a winner. When you believe in yourself and your capacity to do the right thing, this influences people. Others will begin to place their faith in you as a leader. It does not matter whether you are right or wrong; it boils down to people's belief in your capacity to make decisions.

Do people who have an air of self-confidence really know it all? Are they really perfect or do they only appear to be?

It is well known that when we hear something repeatedly, eventually we will believe it to be true.[34] This is the case even if the statement itself is an absurdity or a lie. In World War II, Joseph Goebbels, the Minister of Propaganda of Germany said, "Repeat a lie often enough and it becomes the truth."[35]

Psychological research has shown that, regardless of the truth or credibility of a certain statement, the more we hear it, the more we believe it.[36] This happens even if we did not initially believe it to be true! In psychology, this is known as the "illusion of truth

34 Tom Stafford, "How Liars Create the 'Illusion of truth'," BBC, October 26, 2016, https://www.bbc.com/future/article/20161026-how-liars-create-the-illusion-of-truth.

35 Ibid.

36 Ibid.

effect."[37] Typical lab experiments expose people to phrases and facts, where some are true and some are not. An example is the statement, "a date is a dried plum," which is factually incorrect. After a break of minutes, days, or weeks, those same people are exposed to another set of phrases and facts that are true and false. Some are new statements, while others are from the original set. Over time, after hearing "a date is a dried plum" repeatedly, the mind begins to recognize it as a truth because it has been exposed to that "fact" repeatedly.[38]

The reason this happens so easily is the difficulty of verifying the truth of every single piece of information we consume. It's much easier for us to believe what someone else says with conviction rather than take the time to think it through or research it ourselves. This is especially true if you hear something from what you consider a credible source of information.

Just consider society's feminine beauty ideals. Every few decades, societal beauty standards undergo a drastic change. Realistically speaking, this is too short of a time span for people's preferences to change so drastically. It's that the images shown to us by the media that tell us what society should consider beautiful change.[39] The idea of beauty built by the media has such a tremendous impact on our perception of beauty. Just look at some images of female beauty ideals from the early 1900s and you will see what I mean.

Why is this information relevant to us now, you may ask?

Sophia Loren once said, "The woman who is confident in her

---

37 Ibid.
38 Ibid.
39 Jacqueline Howard, "The History of the 'Ideal' Woman and Where that Has Left Us," CNN, March 9, 2018, https://www.cnn.com/2018/03/07/health/body-image-history-of-beauty-explainer-intl/index.html.

beauty will be able to convince all the others as well."

If you think that you are not good enough, then why would you expect anyone to believe otherwise?

You must believe and trust in yourself and in your attractiveness first. If you are persistent in doing so, other people will believe you too!

If you keep telling yourself how ugly you are and project this message with your behavior, people will eventually believe you, even if they didn't think so initially! But if you proudly embrace who you are, and you let people see that you are indeed precious, unique and one of a kind, then people will approach you in the same way. Believe in yourself. Stand up for yourself. Be proud of yourself and show that to the world! Of course, you shouldn't be conceited, because that's a very unattractive personality trait, but never be ashamed of your strengths and of your true self!

HOW CAN YOU ENHANCE YOUR SELF-CONFIDENCE?

LEARN IT!

Being confident in one area of our lives doesn't automatically mean that we are confident in all areas of life. For example, I am confident in my ability to lead an awesome Beautyrobic class or giving an interesting and informative talk about the topics of this book. However, I'm not sure if someone asked me to swim across the Danube River or to kayak across Lake Tahoe that I would be capable of doing that. My self-confidence would suddenly vanish!

So, where do you go from here?

We all have certain areas where we know our stuff and are truly competent and confident. Confidence comes from competence! If you wish to develop confidence in a certain area, then you should strive to learn more about it and practice it until you become both competent and confident in it. I avoided the phrase "until you become a professional" deliberately, because you don't need to be a professional to have an understanding. You only need to learn and know something at the level that enables you to perform it confidently!

THE 4-PHASE LEARNING PROCESS

Let me give you an example that illustrates this process. Think of the phases of learning to drive a car:

1. No experience. You have never driven a vehicle, no one has ever shown you how to do it, and therefore you have absolutely no idea what it is that you should know. → Unconscious Incompetence.

2. Some demonstration. Someone shows you how to drive. You realize how many things you need to pay attention

to, how many rules there are, and it dawns on you that you will need to learn a lot more than you thought. → Conscious Incompetence.

3. Hands-on experience. You have learned how to drive, but you need to concentrate every time you get in the car. → Conscious Competence.

4. Experienced. Once you have spent more time driving, looking in the mirrors and moving a steering wheel become automatic. → Unconscious Competence.

If there is an area where you don't feel confident, but you wish that you were, work through these levels one by one. By the time you get to Level 4, "Experienced," you can rest assured you will no longer have problems with your self-confidence in that area.

There will always be exceptions to these phases. There are people who will have lots of confidence as early as phase 1, even though they are not proficient. These people believe in themselves and their capacity to learn anything or handle any situation. This self-confidence approach from the aspect of attractiveness is a great thing, even if sometimes they may miss the mark. But if you are anything like me, someone who strives to ensure success and minimize the potential for failure, then I have a solution for you. Practice and keep practicing until you can do something with confidence. This is a technique that works every time and with everybody! The positive effect of being self-assured is that it increases your ability to focus on the purpose of the activity you are doing, which is crucial for efficiency.

There is one more important reason why confidence is so important. When you are confident about something, instead of concentrating on your fears and doubts, you can focus on the goal of the activity. Returning to the previous driving analogy, when you no longer need to pay attention to the technical part of driving, you will then be able to focus on the road and on the direction that you're heading. To give you another example, perhaps you go to a party to meet someone new. If your self-esteem is low, the whole time you will be fixating on how your dress looks, whether your belly looks flat enough, or what other people may be thinking about you. However, if you are self-assured, you are then able to focus your attention on someone of interest. You can flirt, smile, and have a great time. If you do have feelings of low confidence and low self-esteem, take a few meditative breaths and focus on something about yourself that you *are* confident in, whether it is a conversation topic, a physical feature, or something else you have control over. Just by shifting your focus, you'll begin to radiate confidence and feel surer of yourself. Others will notice that and be drawn to you.

Whenever I speak at an event, people are amazed at how professional I sound. This is not because I was born a public speaker, but because I have practiced it so many times that I have mastered my presentation. My early presentations did not go so smoothly, but I practiced it many times and did not give up until I became better.

A few years ago, I was invited to be a guest lecturer at a renowned Hungarian university, and I had prepared my speech in advance. I was asked to talk about marketing techniques for building a successful brand. When I began my presentation, it took me about four minutes to realize that my audience wasn't interested at all in the topic. Most of the students didn't even know if they wanted to become entrepreneurs. The level of my presentation was way too high for them.

This was not the fault of the students. They were not in the same phase of learning as me and didn't have any preliminary training in the subject. Since I am an experienced speaker, I didn't need to pay any attention to my posture or body language, whether my voice was loud enough, etc. Instead, I could devote my full attention to my audience. Because of this, I realized immediately that I couldn't grab their attention with the topic I had prepared.

At that point, I decided to abandon my presentation and change the subject. I asked my audience how many of them were planning to become entrepreneurs. I discovered that only a very few (approximately 3%) of the students wanted to own their own business. Another 3–4 % wanted to become employees. The rest had no clear plans, so I decided to talk about life as an entrepreneur. I spoke about the advantages of becoming an entrepreneur and the positives aspects of owning your own business. At this point, I noticed a shift in the audience and could tell they were interested. My improvised speech was such a tremendous success that a professor congratulated me at the end. He told me that no other guest lecturer had been able to grab their attention to that extent. Had I not been a confident public speaker, I would not have noticed the students' disinterest, or may not have cared, because my focus would have been on saying everything perfectly.

Let me share a secret with you about my Beautyrobic classes. My classes are always full, and I often get feedback from my guests about how much they love to come to them. I can be tough during sessions. I devote my full attention to my clients during the class and the number of repetitions of a given exercise is not previously planned. Instead, I observe my clients' reactions and push their limits outside their comfort zone. Since every class is different, the only way for me to customize each class is to give them my undivided and complete attention. The reason I can devote that kind of attention to each class is because I have held so many classes over the years and developed my skills as an instructor. Thanks to this experience and confidence, I do not need to concentrate on myself.

Once you have dedicated enough practice to a particular skill and built confidence in that area, you will be able to focus on your objective instead of your insecurities or your lack of knowledge. This will increase your chances of reaching your goals successfully!

BELIEVE IN YOURSELF!

Faith in yourself and self-confidence are two of the keys to being attractive and magnetic to other people.

To acquire these traits, you will need two things.

The first is having **healthy self-esteem**. Self-esteem is easily damaged throughout your life and can be very difficult to repair. For example, some people were raised by overly critical parents who belittled them throughout their childhood. Such people were conditioned to believe that they are worthless. The same is true for someone who was constantly scorned and degraded by a romantic partner for years. Several studies have shown that we are heavily influenced by the opinions of the people around us. This phenomenon is known as self-fulfilling prophecy, also called the Pygmalion effect.[40]

An experiment was conducted on this subject by two American researchers, Robert Rosenthal and Lenore Jacobson.[41] They contacted an elementary school with the alleged purpose of having the students take pre-tests for a new intelligence test. They used the tests to choose several average-ability pupils at random. They informed their teachers that the chosen students possessed exceptional potential for intellectual growth, which they expected to surface in their academic achievements. After a year, the researchers returned. They found that the selected students were among the very best in every class. The experiment demonstrated that because the teachers attributed extraordinary potential to these students, their behavior towards these students reflected this belief, and in turn influenced the behavior of these children.[42]

This is a perfect illustration of how much our self-esteem is influenced by other people's behavior towards us and how much our beliefs about ourselves impact our outcomes. If you feel that you are degraded or treated as unworthy by your environment, make a change immediately.

Richard Wiseman is a psychology professor who has also researched the role of self-fulfilling prophecies. He found that those of us who believe that other people are friendly tend to smile more at people, and in response other people smile back at them

---

40 Robert Rosenthal and Lenore Jacobson, *Pygmalion in the Classroom: Teacher Expectation and Pupils' Intellectual Development* (Carmarthen, UK: Crown House Publishing, 2003): 4-5.

41 Ibid.

42 Ibid.

more often.[43] People tend to be more friendly towards them in general. Similarly, those who think of themselves as lucky tend to take chances more often than others and by doing so, they actually boost their chances of winning.[44]

The above examples are the perfect illustrations of the importance of self-esteem. If you are struggling with your self-worth and low self-esteem issues that you have been unable to resolve on your own, I strongly recommend you seek professional help. As long as you are still struggling with self-criticism and self-worth, you will never be able to tap into the full potential of your attractiveness and charisma. There are individual and group therapies that can help you identify the root cause of your self-esteem issues and treat them. It is very important that you take this seriously and if necessary, you address this issue with a professional. If you ignore the problem and don't try to resolve the root cause, then there's no point in reading books or researching methods of self-improvement because you will not be addressing the underlying cause of those issues.

You must believe in yourself and in your own magnetism. If you do, you will have the power to control your self-fulfilling prophecy. When you believe that you are attractive or worthy, you will behave accordingly, and attract other people to you.

43 Karla Starr, "When You Look for Luck, You Get Luckier, Psychology Today, January 31, 2013, https://www.psychologytoday.com/us/blog/the-science-luck/201301/when-you-look-luck-you-get-luckier.

44   Ibid.

RIGHT ATTITUDE

In my experience, another important prerequisite for acquiring self-confidence is having **the right attitude.** There will always be some aspects of life that you cannot change, but you are in control of most aspects of your life. You must be able to take responsibility for what you can. If you are perseverant and confident, sooner or later you will be able to change your circumstances. Living your life with a sense of self-ownership and responsibility is key. This requires you to remove your expectations and blame others for your circumstances. When you accept that you alone are responsible for your life, you take charge of your destiny and then take action to shape it. Before long, you will develop so much self-confidence that it will blow people's minds. This will take practice, but you will gradually develop the habit of changing or correcting the things you have control over, and this will build up a kind of unshakeable self-confidence in you that will make you inescapably attractive to others!

This is crucial, so let's delve into this in more detail.

If you feel that there is an area of your life that you are not confident in, you will need to examine it from the following perspective.

YOU CAN CHANGE VS. YOU CANNOT CHANGE

YOU CANNOT CHANGE SOMETHING BUT CAN MAKE THE BEST OF IT

If you are focused on something you cannot change, you must stop worrying about it, because… C'est la vie! That's the reality of your situation. You must learn to accept it and try to look at it from a different angle! By shifting your perspective, it will no longer cause you suffering.

Consider models who were born with some sort of congenital abnormality. If they let it eat away at their self-confidence, they would never have made it. However, if they learn to accept being different, get over it, and even feel proud of who they are, suddenly everyone else will begin to accept them. Winnie Harlow is a Canadian top model. She was formerly labeled the "dotted" model, but became a role model to millions of teenagers lacking self-confidence. She became a finalist in the *America's Next Top Model* reality series. Winnie happens to have vitiligo, an incurable skin condition that causes pigment loss of the skin, resulting in white patches on her dark skin. But she didn't let that get in her way, no matter how scary this condition may have seemed to others. Winnie has been featured on the covers of all major magazines and walked the catwalk of the most prominent fashion shows.[45] Rebekah Marine is a top model born without a right forearm. Even as a child, she felt that differences should not be hidden but celebrated. Although she was born without a forearm, she didn't let this stop her in any area of her life and she became a successful model.[46]

---

45 Kaitlyn Frey and Emily Strohm, "Making the Cut Star Winnie Harlow on her Supermodel Fame: 'My Plan was Never to Fail'," People, July 22, 2021, https://people.com/style/winnie-harlow-talks-supermodel-fame-plan-never-fail/.

46 Char Adams, "Model Born Without Forearm Faces her Fear of Marriage and Stars on Say Yes to the Dress: 'I Learned to Love Myself First'," People, February 28, 2019, https://people.com/health/rebekah-marine-say-yes-dress-exclusive/.

Sometimes there are things you just can't change about yourself, but suffering and stressing over them won't make them any better. There's one thing you can do in such cases: change your perspective and accept it.

YOU BELIEVE YOU CANNOT CHANGE, BUT YOU *DO* HAVE THE POWER TO CHANGE

Many people erroneously think that it's impossible for them to change their life or their circumstances, so, they don't even try to change it. This phenomenon is called trained incapacity.[47]

Most of us have seen an elephant in the circus or at the zoo, where just a thin rope separates the strong giant from its freedom—and the spectators. The elephant could break that rope with great ease. How come it doesn't even try? The answer is trained incapacity. When circus elephants are still young, they are bound by strong ropes and tied to a bar to keep them locked away. At first, the baby elephant will fight and try to run away and attempt to break the rope, but eventually it will give up. Later, when they are 10 times bigger and stronger, they could break the rope easily, but they don't even attempt to; the rope has become their "insurmountable obstacle."[48]

People often behave the same way. Because of past setbacks, disappointments or negative experiences, we believe a situation or obstacle to be insurmountable, when it is not the case. The question becomes, *why* do you feel a lack of control? If there is a

---

47 John Spacey, "What is Trained Incapacity?" Simplicable, July 8, 2016, https://simplicable.com/new/trained-incapacity.

48 "Baby elephants, Bound and Broken: This is How Circuses Train Elephants," PETA, https://headlines.peta.org/how-circuses-train-baby-elephants/.

constant, internal reason behind it (for example, negative self-talk such as, "I am a failure at everything I do. I have always been like this, and I will never change"), then you will have a hard time trying new things.

However, there are people who always blame other people or external forces for all their failures, and they believe that what happens in their lives is out of their control. They think that every event influencing their lives occurs independently of them and they don't assume any responsibility. These individuals are called outer-directed people.[49] They tend to think that they have no power over things, therefore they don't even take action to try to take control of their lives.[50]

One of my favorite quotes attributed to Albert Einstein is, "Everybody knows a certain thing is unrealizable until somebody unaware of this comes and invents it."[51]

History has proven time and time again that impossible is not a fact, it's an opinion.[52] This is why I ask you to never assume something is impossible. If you have a strong desire to do something, don't give up on it.

---

49 Gabriel Lopez-Garrido, "Locus of Control," Simply Psychology, September 13, 2020, https://www.simplypsychology.org/locus-of-control.html.

50 American psychologist Julian Rotter suggested that in the course of social learning people develop a belief as to whether certain events that occur to them are consequences of their own behavior vs. isolated, accidental events outside our control. Based on this assumption, he distinguished between the internal and external locus of control.

51 Mohsen Ibrahim and Beatrice Trabalza Marinucci, "Commentary: When Spontaneous Means Threatening. The Importance of Thinking Differently to Prevent an Unexpected, Severe Event," *JTCVS* 7 (June 2021): 306. https://doi.org/10.1016/j.xjtc.2021.02.007.

52 Adam Dachis, "Impossible is Not a Fact. It's an Opinion," Life Hacker, June 4, 2012, https://lifehacker.com/impossible-is-not-a-fact-its-an-opinion-5915568.

YOU BELIEVE YOU CAN CHANGE IT, BUT IT CAN'T BE CHANGED

Those who think that every event in their life derives exclusively from their own actions are called people with strong internal locus of control.[53] Naturally, this personal character trait has lots of advantages. This individual knows that their life is in their hands, and they can shape how it turns out. They assume responsibility for their own lives and actions.

But there are situations in life where the person who thinks that they are in control is wrong.

I tend to think that I have everything under my control. We must realize that there are situations that we cannot influence, no matter how much we want to. This was the case with my wedding. When we were planning our third wedding (because my husband and I chose to have three celebrations), there was one thing I couldn't control: the weather.

We planned to hold a beautiful outdoor ceremony and host our guests amidst breathtaking lake scenery. We were supposed to say our sweet vows by a flowery lake altar against the backdrop of a summer sunset. Instead, we had the harshest day of the entire summer. The temperature fell 20 degrees from one day to the next, and after a sudden cloud burst, massive amounts of rain fell all day long. At first, I was overcome with a feeling of total despair. After a while, I had to accept that there was really nothing I could do about it. So, I gathered my wits, shook it off, and decided that despite the weather, we would make it the best wedding ever for our guests. We crammed everyone into the wedding tent for the ceremony and the dinner. My husband and I threw such a terrific

---

53 Lopez-Garrido, "Locus of Control."

party that our guests had the time of their lives while celebrating our marriage.

The shift came when I started to focus on the positive aspects of the unavoidable bad weather. The rain ultimately kept everyone together. Our wedding guests were united in one place, instead of being scattered about. Everyone was able to socialize, and the dance floor was packed. It helped to remind myself of the saying that rain on your wedding day is good luck! Focusing on these thoughts made me feel better. Despite the bad weather, it was the most beautiful day of my life!

YOU CAN CHANGE IT

Most things *can* be changed! Some things may seem impossible at first, but you can do it. Read the valuable advice in this section carefully, and don't forget to put everything into practice.

Don't procrastinate! Tackle every important problem head on. I know it's scary. I know that you are outside your comfort zone but do it anyway and go for it! What's the worst that can happen? The worst-case scenario is that you don't make it. So what? If you don't succeed, at least you learned something from the experience. There is no such thing as failure; there are only opportunities to learn!

The greatest lessons that I have ever learned did not happen when I was succeeding or when I was at the top of my game. I've learned most from the times I failed. Those who think that the opposite of success is failure have it all wrong. Failure is the building block of success. There's only one person who never fails: the one who never steps out of their comfort zone, settles for who they are and never tries to be more.

Consider how a baby learns to walk. Are they going to get up and start running the first time? No! They will stand up, fall down and then try again. They will stand up and fall down, over and over. They will keep repeating it until they can stay upright for a number of steps, then gradually improve until eventually they are comfortable walking, and later to run and jump. This is the human process of learning. The problem is that the go-getter spirit in us often dies as early as childhood. Failing is uncool. It's upsetting when something fails, and we normally avoid what makes us feel bad. It's human nature! If you burn your hand on the stove once, you will never touch a hot stove again. If you have ever experienced how it feels to fall short of achieving what you want so badly and how much pain it causes, the chances are that you will cut and run at the next opportunity to try that same thing again.

But this is not the right mindset. You must try again if you want to become self-assured and successful. And remember: failure is a good thing. It is the price you pay for gaining knowledge and experience. It's intimidating to attempt something when it's brand new or when you've failed at it before, but you must overcome that fear. Failure is not the opposite of success but a building block towards it! Let that sink in.

TECHNIQUES FOR OVERCOMING FEAR

There are a number of ways to help you overcome your fears as you face new challenges in life. These are based on my own experience and will help calm you in a time of need.

When I'm very anxious about something, before I face that situation, I take deep breaths and I imagine that an invigorating energy is refueling me. This energy fills me up with every breath

I take. At the same time, I clench my fists and tell myself, "I'm gonna make it, no matter what!" If possible, before I undertake a task that fills me with anxiety, I listen to some music that fills me up with strength, energy and a zest for life until I feel unstoppable.

It may also help to visualize a successful outcome. Before I get on stage to speak, I imagine the outcome I am trying to achieve. I imagine that everybody is actively listening while I speak and at the end, they clap and cheer. This allows me to feel confident, as if I have already won over my audience before I even step onto the stage. So, visualize your success, see it in your mind's eye, and you will act as confidently as if you have already succeeded!

When I am in the middle of a situation that scares me, I straighten my back and square my shoulders. I breathe evenly and I smile broadly. I try to act self-assured, even if I'm scared stiff inside. This works! Believe it or not, I actually start to feel more self-confident, even though it began as mere acting. It's like when you are pretending to laugh, and after a while you end up genuinely laughing yourself silly and then can't stop.

If you feel anxious or unsure frequently, try to consider that anxiety is not necessarily a bad thing. Experts recognize two kinds of anxiety. There is debilitating anxiety, like anxiety disorders, which decreases and hinders performance and has a paralyzing effect on you. Then there is facilitating anxiety, which enhances and activates performance. While the former distracts and make you feel inadequate, the latter prepares you by generating the optimal level of excitement necessary to cope with stress.[54] For

---

54 Ahmad A. Kader, "Debilitating and facilitating test anxiety and student motivation and achievement in principles of microeconomics," *International Review or Economics Education* 23 (September 2016): 40. https://doi.org/10.1016/j.iree.2016.07.002.

example, this is especially true when taking exams. It's not a stretch to say that facilitating anxiety can even help your performance, compared to someone who experiences no stress at all.[55]

I have found this next stress management technique particularly helpful. I learned this in London at the Millionaire Mind Intensive seminar of T. Harv Eker.[56] It has had a massive impact on me.

I used to think that fear was a bad thing because it often paralyzed me. I've got to admit that I envied the fearless risk-takers who seemed to jump into things and see success in a flash. They appeared to overflow with confidence and an air that they were unstoppable and no challenge could derail their plans. I used to feel that this fearlessnesss was the characteristic that made them born for success and was what drove them. "It's easy for them," I would think to myself.

Then, at this seminar, I heard something that changed everything for me! It was said that there is no such thing as a fearless person because fear is a normal human emotion. It is hardwired into our brains and is an indispensable instinct for our survival. It will trigger in our brains whenever new or unknown things may present a threat. Every human being experiences fear, which disproves the idea that successful people are successful because they don't feel fear. What makes the difference is that successful people act *despite* their fear. Despite their fear, they dive into the task at hand, resolved to succeed, and they pull it off.

---

55 Katherine H. Moyer, "Debilitating and Facilitating Anxiety Effects on Identification," *Journal of Undergraduate Psychological Research* 3 (2008): 6. http://citeseerx.ist.psu.edu/viewdoc/download?doi=10.1.1.537.414&rep=rep1&type=pdf

56 "T. Harv Eker: Millionaire Mind Intensive – Introduction," Success Resources Australia, YouTube, November 18, 2013, https://www.youtube.com/watch?v=JI8ha-eJTxk.

The technique I learned for combatting fear goes as follows. The next time you are facing something that scares you, realize and acknowledge that you are experiencing the feeling of fear. Take a moment to thank your mind for warning you of the perceived threat, then dive into what you have resolved to do.

Do the things that fill you with fear, and eventually they will become natural to you. When you do something well, continue to step up your game and improve, so that eventually you will find yourself among the best at that skill. Once you have checked one thing off your list, go to the next thing, and don't give up until you have conquered that one too. Continue this practice with the next thing and the next. Make a habit of this! Over time, you will realize that you can achieve anything if you persevere. This practice will give you an inner strength and self-confidence that everyone around you will notice.

DATING AND CONFIDENCE

When you are on a date, it's important to pay attention to your date rather than being distracted by your self-doubt. Focusing on yourself in a negative way will make you appear distracted and uncomfortable.

Let's take a look at the reasons you may not be self-confident in dating.

APPEARANCE

If you are insecure about your body, simply work on it, and it will increase your self-esteem! If you're wearing a dress that you love your body in, you will become more confident. If you put on some seductive, sexy lingerie, you will feel more powerful. Why? Because it's not only our inner state that affects our appearance, but also how we appear on the outside. You will be much more self-confident when you feel like you look great. It's important that you wear an outfit and a pair of shoes you look good *and* feel amazing in. No matter how good it looks, if it makes you feel uncomfortable, you will be preoccupied with this uneasy feeling the whole date, instead of dedicating your attention to the other person.

TRUST YOURSELF

If you are afraid of not being good enough for the other person, I have advice for you. Be yourself, and if the other person doesn't like it, let it be their problem! Don't try to live up to the expectations of the other person, don't try to guess what your date likes or be what you think they want. Show them who you truly are! In the long run, it's impossible to pretend that you are someone else, so what's the point in doing so to begin with? I'm not absolving you from the responsibility of working on yourself and striving to be a better version of yourself. However, pretending that you are a different person is never a wise thing to do, and will only make you seem uncomfortable.

If there is someone who dislikes the way you are, learn to stand up for yourself! You will have critics, but no matter what you do, be yourself. People will always form an opinion about everything, but you mustn't concern yourself with them. You will never be able to please everybody! Let people criticize you for your true self rather than appreciating you for who you are pretending to be. If you project a fake image of yourself to the world, you will attract the wrong kind of people, and the best people will pass you by. Don't be afraid, and don't let fear have the upper hand.

The more impact you have on those around you, the more critics you will have. You must learn to distinguish between constructive and destructive criticism. Most criticism is irrelevant. There are many people who would rather spend their time criticizing others than create something themselves. Don't let them affect you; just be yourself and don't concern yourself with who likes you and who doesn't.

PRACTICE MAKES PERFECT!

The way to become self-confident in dating works the same way as anything else. In other words, the best approach here is to practice until it comes naturally to you. This will allow you to let go of your nerves and uneasiness and you will be able to dedicate your attention to your date. You will become a genuinely sexy, attractive and confident woman who sweeps dates off their feet.

THE CONFIDENT WOMAN

I often get the impression that people confuse self-assurance with authoritarian decisiveness. This can work in certain situations— in business, for example, you can achieve some results with this attitude. But it could drive a man, friends or coworkers away from you. Being a confident woman does not mean clinging to your arguments rigidly and aggressively. Confidence is not acting like you are above others, being better and more beautiful than others, or knowing everything. Confidence is knowing your strengths, values and the qualities that make you, *you*.

At the same time, a confident woman is mindful of her weaknesses and accepts them. She is aware that she doesn't have to be perfect to be loved. She doesn't constantly require external validation to feel worthwhile. When she wants to achieve something, she doesn't procrastinate or look for excuses, but leaps into action. She's not afraid to take risks, because she knows that she is capable of more.

A confident woman doesn't care about what other people think, because she knows that not everyone is going to like her. She won't let disappointments stop her and will go beyond her comfort zone. She isn't comparing herself to others because she is busy seeking to improve and develop herself. She looks for quality in relationships rather than quantity.

The confident woman doesn't constantly expect help from others but does things for herself. She faces inconveniences and obstacles courageously, and when she falls, she rises back up. A strong, confident woman has the courage to embrace her soft side and will defer to her partner when necessary. It doesn't pose an ego problem for her because confidence does not have to mean dominance.

In short, a confident woman believes in herself, no matter what happens!

This is exactly what will give you an air of magnetism that will attract all eyes to you as you enter a room. It will make you so irresistible that everybody will want to be around you. You can reach this level of confidence, even if you feel that it is unattainable right now. Start applying the advice I'm giving you in this book consciously and you will notice a change in yourself, in your life and in your attractiveness!

EXERCISES

Write a list of all the things you have not done because of fear, despite it being important to you! Arrange them in order of difficulty. Start with the easiest task, and then tackle them one by one. I know that you have fears that will take you a while to overcome. But don't give up, continue to face them until they no longer scare you.

❊

Make a list of the self-fulfilling prophecies you hold about yourself. The negative ones will stand in the way of your success and even your charisma, so start replacing them consciously.

For example, you may feel that you are not likeable. Change it.

Make it your resolution to become likeable from now on. Start making a conscious effort to behave in a way that will make other people like you. Be generous to others. Use kind words. Smile at them.

Change only one thing at a time, and when you're done, move on to the next one.

Make a list of things that stand in the way of your magnetism and then group them into to the following categories:

- ▸ Things I cannot change
- ▸ Things I can change

Reconsider whether it really belongs in the group you put it in. You can even show it to a friend and ask them what they think. Perhaps there is something you can change that you believed that you couldn't, or vice versa. Remember the story of the elephant.

Once you have identified the categories, read through the appropriate passage of this chapter once more to see what you need to do about the things you cannot change and about the things you can.

Start practicing Beautyrobic workouts. They are not only excellent for full-body toning and fat-burning, but they help you to increase your self-confidence and self-love.

chapter five

LEVEL IV: B.A.G.

YOU'VE GOT IT IN THE B.A.G!

Attracting others is not something you can force. You can't make others feel attracted to you by clinging to them or pushing yourself on them. It's you that must practice the magic and change yourself into the most attractive version of yourself if you want to see results. Picture yourself like a magnet that will have massive power if it increases its own strength. If the magnet is not strong enough, then no matter how hard we try, it won't attract other metallic objects. In this chapter, we are going to increase your appeal. Read the following lines very carefully, because if you understand what I'm saying, it will dramatically change your life for the better!

This book offers a solution for bringing out the maximum charisma in yourself. I am not giving you a one-size-fits-all solution. I don't want you to be a trend follower or a uniform woman. On the contrary... I want to help you open your eyes to see and treasure the incredible attractiveness that you have within you. Every single woman is fantastic, but most of them will never tap into their full potential.

It's as if you had a treasure chest buried in your garden but had no idea that it was there. You would continue to live your whole life without ever bringing it to the surface. Or when you have a smartphone with lots of features, but you only use a few and never teach yourself how to use the rest.

I want to bring to the surface your colorful character, individuality, inner femme fatale and true attractiveness! I want you to show the world who you truly are, and what it's like when you shine your light. What you can achieve is much bigger than what you have ever dared to imagine.

Let's talk about how to do this with B.A.G. It is an acronym for the following three words:

B: Balance
A: Awareness
G: Growth

These three letters spell out the word B.A.G. Out of all the levels, this is among the most important ones, so I wanted this to be easy to memorize, and I have yet to meet a woman who doesn't love bags!

We've got to tend to and care for this level just as much as we love adorable bags. This is the level that is hardest to achieve. It must be sustained, which requires constant effort, lots of work and plenty of energy. But in turn, this is the level that will bring about the most radical change in your life.

Why is this?

To become magnetic to other people, you first need to learn to accept yourself, love yourself, and find your inner harmony. You must create balance within yourself and in your life. You must know who you are, what your strengths and values are, and cherish yourself and your personality. You should respect and love yourself enough to be able to accept good things and know that you deserve them.

You should know that you are a precious, valuable person who deserves to be loved, and who deserves to be a beautiful, charming, irresistible and fulfilled woman. It's not enough if you simply know it, you should also believe that you deserve these things and do whatever it takes to achieve them! Love yourself and find the balance within the different areas of your life. Stop comparing yourself continuously to others. Don't envy anyone else. Enjoy your uniqueness and being different! Your task is not to become perfect, because there's no such thing. You've got to maximize your own true attractiveness and tap into your full potential.

Why do I stress this so much?

Because we women often get into situations and relationships that are less than what we deserve and put up with things we shouldn't. The reason is that deep down, we are not in harmony with ourselves, don't love ourselves, don't believe in ourselves and are unaware of our own value and worth.

How many women end up continually attracting the wrong kind of men into their lives? How many women drift through life and resign themselves to whatever it happens to throw at them (whether in work, love or other areas of life) instead of taking control? How many women don't respect and love themselves, lack inner balance or don't know they are worthy of love? All of that will have serious repercussions on their circumstances, conditions, human relationships and on their whole life. If you don't respect and love yourself, if you don't believe that you are attractive and worthy of love, how can you expect anyone else to?

"If you change the way you look at things,
the things you look at change."
— Dr. Wayne W. Dyer[57]

B FOR BALANCE

If you want to create balanced human relationships in your life and become charismatic to people around you, you must find the balance within you as well as in different areas of your life. Never let your inner balance depend on external circumstances!

Picture a tightrope walker who can maintain their balance and preserve their stability, despite the rope beneath their feet swinging and swaying. No matter how thin the rope or how distracting the surroundings, nothing can make them lose their balance! Similarly,

---

57 "If You Change the Way You Look at Things, the Things You Look at Change," Philosoblog, October 10, 2013, https://philosiblog.com/2013/10/10/if-you-change-the-way-you-look-at-things-the-things-you-look-at-change/.

a woman who is in perfect harmony with herself will manage to preserve it in the face of external instability. She will remain grounded even if she finds herself in a group of negative people who try to drag her down, and even if she happens to have a man in her life who is not the right one for her.

Remember what I said earlier: you can't control external influences, but you can change and control yourself and get yourself in balance. The more grounded you are, the more you are in harmony with yourself, the less vulnerable you will be to external events. Negative people and bad news will always be there and there's nothing you can do about it. What will make all the difference is the way that you react. Imagine walking in the rain while holding a giant umbrella in your hand. No matter how much it rains, you will stay completely dry. Similarly, when you have achieved inner balance, although negative things will continue to be there, you will be completely immune to them.

To reach this state of balance, you've got to examine your life in the following areas:

Balance:

- ▶ Balance with yourself (body/mind/soul)

- ▶ Balance with your surroundings/environment (social environment/living environment)

- ▶ Balance between your feminine roles (partner/lover/mother/career woman)

- ▶ Balance with your feminine energy

IN BALANCE WITH YOURSELF
• BODY, MIND, SOUL •

BODY

I mentioned earlier that one of my favorite quotes is, "Work out because you love your body, not because you hate it!"

Think of your body as the castle that you live in and treat it accordingly. Take good care of it. Eat a healthy diet, and always give your body adequate exercise. It's great if you push yourself to the limit of your abilities, since all progress takes place when we step out of our comfort zone, but you must use a commonsense approach. What matters is your attitude! Try to accept your figure, work to improve your overall health and strive to bring out the best in your natural features. But most importantly, learn to love, respect and get into balance with it.

Many people make the mistake of chasing an ideal body type that is incompatible with their own genetics or bone structure, instead of considering their own physical characteristics and getting the most out of their own bodies. You've got to bring the best out of your *own* body type. Every body shape is beautiful if we take care of it, get it into shape and bring out its best attributes! You should make this your objective. You should try to bring out the best from it. In Level 1, I wrote about the techniques to achieve this in more detail. Turn back, if you need to, and read it again.

EXERCISES

Try to look at your body through a fresh pair of eyes. Think of it as something you must take care of. What good things would you do for it? What nutrients would you use to nurture it? Try to embrace yourself and your body. View it as one of your most precious treasures!

Research the various body shapes (sandglass, pear, rectangle/banana, apple, and inverted triangle/strawberry, or according to the somatotypes, ectomorph, mesomorph and endomorph) and identify which of these categories you belong in.[58] Find a woman who you think has managed to get the most out the same body type you have. It can be an actress or a singer if you like. Look at how she dresses, what traits she accentuates, and make it your goal to replicate it! You can even do a quick Internet search for "flattering styles for [insert body type here]" to find clothing cuts, styles and colors that fit your body shape best.

MIND

You are often told how important it is to go to the gym or get regular exercise because that's the way to keep your body healthy

---

58 "The 3 Body Types: Ectomorph, Mesomorph, & Endomorph," Wellnessed, accessed 6/7/22, https://wellnessed.com/body-types/.

and achieve optimal functioning of your muscles. However, our brain works the same way. It will work properly only for those who exercise it and put it to work.

It helps to imagine your brain as a muscle. Regardless of whether someone was born with great natural abilities, if they don't train regularly, they will become weak and ineffective. Even if you were born with natural intelligence, if you don't strive to improve and challenge yourself, with time your brain may weaken and your intellect may be wasted. Conversely, someone who wasn't born a genius but consistently learns and trains their brain will surpass those who may have been born smarter but chose not to utilize and expand their intelligence.[59] We've got to train our brains regularly and challenge our intelligence continuously. We should never stop learning, even when we complete school or after retirement.

WHY IS THIS RELEVANT TO BEING ATTRACTIVE?

Intelligence is astonishingly intriguing! A smart woman is extremely charismatic and interesting. Naturally, you begin a conversation when you meet a new person. If you can share your views and opinions on any subject in an intelligent and well-informed manner, it makes you more interesting to the other person. More importantly, this will not just make you interesting in the short term, but you'll be able to capture and keep people's attention for the long run too!

External beauty is captivating but can become boring over time. A smart woman who can have a substantial, meaningful

---

59 Robert J. Sternberg, "Increasing Fluid Intelligence is Possible After All," *PNAS* 105, no. 19 (May 2008): 6791, https://doi.org/10.1073/pnas.0803396105.

conversation is able to sustain interest long-term. You will feel the difference in conversation. It will flow more smoothly, feel more natural and never get stale or awkward.

Your ability to fit in and assert yourself in a group setting is also determined largely by your intelligence. The smarter you are, the easier it will be for you to join people's conversations and to attract positive attention towards you. This is especially true for people who also have a higher-than-average EQ.[60]

A while ago, I attended a business gala where I was introduced to a person in a very high position who was also one of the keynote speakers. I knew where he worked and had read about the goals of his organization. When we met, I told him where I thought he made a mistake and in what ways he could improve to achieve what he wanted. Not only did he incorporate my ideas into his speech, but after the event, he sought me out to offer me a job on his team.

I believe this happened for two reasons:

▶ The things I said to him were meaningful and added value to his organization. He recognized my intelligence and competence.

▶ I was wearing a beautiful evening gown, and my overall look was attractive.

These two things made me so captivating that, although this person was normally unapproachable in everyday life, he made a point to find me and offer me a job.

---

60 Kendra Cherry, "What is Emotional Intelligence?" Verywell Mind, June 3, 2020, https://www.verywellmind.com/what-is-emotional-intelligence-2795423.

My appearance alone would not have achieved this result! Although I looked very pretty that night, there were many other pretty ladies there. Physical appearance alone won't make anyone stand out from the crowd. However, a beautiful woman with brilliant thoughts… well, that's a killer combination!

SENSE OF HUMOR

Your sense of humor may just be your secret weapon for attracting others. Humor is closely related to intelligence.[61] Our sense of humor shows the level of one's intelligence, creativity and social competence because it demonstrates abstract thinking. In addition, you need intelligence to understand satire and subtle jokes. So, whether you are the joker or the listener, it takes intelligence and cognitive flexibility to have a good sense of humor!

ENJOY LEARNING

Learning has always been important to me, even though I wasn't exactly an exceptionally talented or extremely brilliant kid when I first started going to school. With hard work, I managed to be among one of the best pupils. I then received scholarships at the highest levels in college. After graduation, I never stopped learning and studying. I was always open to acquiring new skills and new information.

Over the years, I have continued to broaden my knowledge even more intensely and consciously. This practice has continued to benefit me in many areas of my life. Today, I receive invitations

---

61 Gil Greengross and Geoffrey Miller, "Humor Ability Reveals Intelligence, Predicts Mating Success, and is Higher in Males," *Intelligence* 39 (2011): 188, https://doi.org/10.1016/j.intell.2011.03.006.

from universities and conferences to hold lectures and make a living by sharing my knowledge. For years, I haven't had a boss. I became my own boss.

This is relevant because intelligence is one of the pillars of my attractiveness. Men and women equally respect me and like to be around me. I know that I earned their respect thanks to the intelligence I built from learning.

When I tell you to develop your mind, please don't think of it as traditional schooling! There are many other ways to learn new things. Find the method that's optimal for you and incorporate it into your life by adding it to your schedule. Today, money is rarely an obstacle to learning. There's a vast amount of knowledge available for everyone. Books, audiobooks, podcasts, online trainings, YouTube and other video sites, blogs and social media sites are just some of the sources. So many useful lectures, tutorials, and materials are available easily for everyone.

I personally recommend TED Talks, not only because they contain intelligent discussions on a wide range of topics, but also because they are very inspiring.

Don't think of learning as something bad that you are forced to do to get a good grade. Be curious and thirsty for knowledge! When you come across something you don't understand, look it up and have an open mind for new information. Try to think of learning as something enjoyable. Go to the theater, visit exhibitions or museums and try to find forms of entertainment that aren't just mindlessly enjoyable, but are enjoyable in a way that exercises the mind.

EXERCISE

Each month, go and participate in an exciting program or activity that trains your mind. This may be anything from an exhibition to a theater play. The only thing that matters is that it not only entertains you, but also challenges your intellect. Plan one such activity for yourself every month!

SOUL

Getting into balance with your own soul, accepting the way you are, loving yourself and understanding your own reactions and thoughts is very important. Do not indulge in hatred, but approach people and situations with an open mind and positive spirit. These are all ways to bring your soul into balance!

Indulging in negativity and hate will only hold you back. If you are not happy with your life, don't try to make others miserable by dragging them down. Instead, take care of yourself and make changes to your own life! Wickedness and callousness are never attractive. All you will achieve with these attitudes is that people will only tolerate you when they have no other choice!

Those who are bitter, unkind, mean, malicious and ungenerous will never be interesting or charismatic to anyone. Unfortunately, many people are resentful and blame their mistakes on others. They are constantly on the lookout for an opportunity to mess with someone else. These types of people criticize and focus on other people's shortcoming. You should not aspire to be one of those people! It will only make you ugly and repulsive to others. Also, when you focus your attention on someone else, you divert it away from you and from your own life. If you must point your finger at somebody, make sure it is at yourself.

I know that very often it is easier to hate someone else rather than to assume responsibility for your own thoughts, feelings and circumstances. The logic behind that is simple—if we are busy finding fault with others, we don't need to account for our own defects. But this won't get us anywhere, especially when it comes to our magnetism.

There is a way, however, to turn your criticism of others into an advantage toward our personal development. You will find out how, during the following exercise:

EXERCISE

Compile a list all the characteristics that you find annoying or repulsive in other people.

Once you know what you don't like in others, you can understand where you are not in balance yourself. If there's something repressed inside you, something you are unwilling to face, it will continue to affect your personality. In psychology, this phenomenon is called the shadow self.[62] Whatever it is that we find upsetting or loathsome about others, it forms part of the shadow self in our personality. The role of the other person we hate is nothing more than a reflection of the traits we hate in ourselves.

---

62 "Carl Jung and the Shadow: The Hidden Power of Our Dark Side," Academy of Ideas, December 17, 2015, https://academyofideas. com/2015/12/carl-jung-and-the-shadow-the-hidden-power-of-our-dark-side/.

GIVE!

Try helping someone purely for the sake of altruism. Donate to an organization, or just do something good for someone spontaneously (it can be as little as saying a kind word) and without any expectations of anything in return. Afterwards, don't simply observe how happy you have made that person but feel the feelings it has sparked within you. What effect does it have on you? I hope that you will feel how wonderful it is to give to others! Altruism, charity and giving are reoccurring themes in a lot of religious and spiritual practices, which are designed to feed and grow the soul. You don't have to be religious or spiritual to believe that being kind and giving to others has a positive impact on your internal balance.

I love Beautyrobic so much because it allows me to give to people and help them have a better, happier life. When I receive messages that I have changed someone's life, they change my life too just by saying so. They make me happy! This reciprocal giving and taking gives us both wings. I believe that this is an indispensable tool in a balanced life.

EXERCISE

Today, do something good for another person at least three times, without any reason! This can be as little as saying a nice word. I leave it to your creativity.
Then watch how it will make you feel.

SELF-LOVE

Earlier, I wrote that you should accept other people and not to be ill-willed towards anyone. This applies not only to other people (and other living beings), but also to yourself! Self-acceptance and self-love are key factors to charisma and happiness. Loving yourself comes from within, from your own heart and soul. You cannot achieve self-love without your soul being in harmony.

I will stress again that desiring to become someone else won't bring you joy or make you charismatic. You are already equipped with a beautiful body, a complex mind, unique hobbies, great personality traits and your own thoughts and ideas. Your objective should be to become the best possible version of yourself using what you already have. Try to accept and love yourself! Respect your unique personality! Value the fact that you are different and bring out your maximum potential! Be the best version of *yourself.* What's most important is that you love yourself. Celebrate and reward yourself for the big and little accomplishments you achieve. This is a great way to start building confidence and self-love. The best praise comes from within.

At Beautyrobic, there is a move where we run our hands along our own bodies and caress it. It's shocking for me to see in how this seemingly simple gesture provokes inhibitions in many women, and how many of them are unable to do it. They are unable to caress and love themselves.

Many of us underestimate or are overly critical of ourselves. I believe our primary objective should be to get to know ourselves deeply and learn to love ourselves. How can you expect other people to give you love if you are unable to love yourself? Getting to know and understand yourself on a deep level connects you with your soul. If you start doing things to bring out your best out qualities, then you will begin to love and have respect for yourself! Of course, I know this is easier said than done.

Let me give you a few exercises that will help you start.

EXERCISES

Set a goal for yourself, and when you reach it, don't forget to praise and reward yourself!

For example, decide that you will pay attention to eating healthy food for an entire week. If you succeed in achieving this resolution, be proud of yourself. Continue for one more week, and another, and another, and after the fourth week, celebrate yourself and your resistance by treating yourself with a reward.

Stand in front of the mirror and, for at least 5 minutes, look into your own eyes and try to notice and grow fond of the special person you are. Love yourself the way you are! Don't focus on the flaws, but on how special and unique you are! Practice this exercise at least three times a week for two months.

Try Beautyrobic and come closer and closer to the mirror week by week. Appreciate how beautiful you are and embrace your femininity.

IN BALANCE WITH YOUR ENVIRONMENT

SOCIAL ENVIRONMENT

The longest study on happiness was conducted by Harvard University.[63] It lasted for 75 years and involved 724 persons. About 60 of them are still alive. The study tracked the lives of two groups of men; the first group started in the study when they were sophomores at Harvard University, and the second was a group of boys from Boston's poorest neighborhoods. The study sought to answer this question: "What keeps us happy as we go through life?" Just like young people today, when these young people were asked this question, they answered that to have a good life, they would need to get rich and famous. However, this 75-year study produced a very different result. The study pointed out clearly and unequivocally that good relationships keep us happier and healthier than wealth or fame.[64] The secret to a happy and fulfilled life is the quantity and quality of our social connections. People who are more socially connected to family, friends and their community, and whose relationships are warm and loving are much happier and physically healthier than people who are isolated. This study has found that to get into balance with yourself and your life, you *must* have an adequate number of close relationships, and what

---

63 Melanie Curtin, "This 75-Year Harvard Study Found the 1 Secret to Leading a Fulfilling Life: Here's Some Wisdom Gleaned from One of the Longest Longitudinal Studies Ever Conducted," Inc., February 27, 2017, https://www.inc.com/magazine/202205/tom-foster/mark-cuban-cold-email-mentor-investor.html. Error: This is an incorrect link!

64 Ibid.

matters even more is the quality of these relationships.[65]

It is your choice who you surround yourself with. Perhaps you can't choose your family, but you can choose your friends. Your life will never be in balance if your negative environment constantly drags you down. You must change it! If you leave your job every day fighting back tears because your coworkers drained all your energy, you need to change your job as soon as possible, or at least transfer to a different department within the organization. If your friends don't lift you up or the people around you don't support you but distress and depress you, it's time to surround yourself with new company.

This is also true of your virtual environment! If someone is making you feel bad on a social media platform, unfollow them or block them. Never let your energy be pulled down, because not only will your mood get worse, but it will negatively affect your radiance and your charisma.

Your life is your responsibility. Do what it takes to make it the best you possibly can!

LIVING ENVIRONMENT

You wouldn't believe how impactful your surroundings are in determining whether you will find the balance and harmony you need. Get your home in order! It is not important because of what others think, but because *you* have to live there. Your home shouldn't just be a place to live, but a place that is a pleasure to come back to every day. It should be an environment that recharges your batteries, sparks joy, gives you good vibes, helps you wind down and relax and brings balance to your life. The same applies to your working environment. Try to create a pleasant atmosphere

---

65 Ibid.

as much as you can, given that you probably spend 8 to 10 hours there every workday.

Our surroundings affect our mood, which is why it is so important that they radiate warmth and tranquility. When we ask the frequent visitors of the Beautyrobic Center why they like it so much, one of the main reasons they cite is the cozy and homely atmosphere. In fact, one of the main advantages of Beautyrobic is that we put a lot of emphasis on the atmosphere in the room.

People can't always tell why, but they feel it when a place gives them good vibes. They are attracted to those places and return whenever they can. It's no wonder that Feng Shui has become so fashionable and popular in interior design!

Marie Kondo, the author of *The Life-Changing Magic of Tidying Up* cast a new light on organizing your home. [66] By getting our living space in order, our life will also become more orderly. If you follow the suggestions of Kondo's book step by step, you will not only save time, energy and stress, but eventually you will also feel relieved. It is no wonder it has become a bestselling book.

Six of Marie Kondo's tips for tidying, organization and leading a better life include:

▸ Tackle one category at a time–laundry, dishes, makeups, etc.

▸ Make a home for everything you own.

▸ Be thankful to your things and your space every day.

▸ Tidy by category, not location.

---

66 Marie Kondo, *The Life-Changing Magic of Tidying Up: The Japanese Art of Decluttering and* Organizing (Berkeley, CA: Ten Speed Press, 2014).

- ▸ Always keep your mind on the end goal.

- ▸ When you assess an object you own, ask yourself if it sparks joy.[67]

To bring your life in balance, it is imperative that you create harmony in your living space. Pay attention to cleanliness, air out the room regularly and surround yourself with beautiful plants and flowers to ensure that there is always fresh air and a good smell. Do everything you can to create a positive and warm atmosphere around you!

BALANCING YOUR FEMININE ROLES

• CAREER WOMAN, MOTHER, PARTNER, LOVER •

There is another very important aspect of balance that we need to discuss. How can you, as a woman, find the right balance between your different feminine roles?

Throughout this section and the next one I will use the terms "masculine energy" and "feminine energy." Feminine energy is defined as creative and inspiring, intuitive and empathetic,

---

67 Ibid.

intelligent and loving.[68] Feminine energy is nurturing and supportive. Being strong in your feminine energy means you are strongly connected to your body and intuition. It is receptive energy and means you can make decisions based on what you feel in your heart.

Masculine energy is about taking action. It is protective and desires to fix problems. Masculine energy is self-confident, strong, and competitive. It can be logical and likes to build, win and break through barriers. When balanced, masculine energy is practical and visionary.[69]

You can see how different feminine and masculine energies are and how each have their strengths and benefits.

Throughout these sections, you'll learn how women should be strong in their feminine energy to maximize their potential in all their roles. A woman not only needs to find her inner balance to unify her body, mind and soul, but also her various roles in life. She must find a balance in her roles as a partner, lover, mother and career woman. It is important that none of our roles suppress any of the others and that we maintain harmony between them.

Of course, there are seasons in life where one of your roles takes precedence over the others, which could temporarily throw

---

68 Bonnie Sadigh, "The Masculine and Feminine Energies and the Role They Play in Your Relationship," Wheel of Wellbeing, 2019, https://wheelofwellbeing.com/the-power-of-energies/.

69 Ibid.

you off balance. This could be the case when becoming a mother for the first time. However, outside of such periods, you should strive to maintain balance between the different roles for the sake of your own harmony and balance, which strongly affects your attractiveness too.

Moreover, the proportion between them may vary not only depending on the various periods of your life, but also from person to person. Listen to your own feelings, and don't let the trends tell you what it is you should do. Social expectations often hold people down. Every one of us is different and what makes me happy, what is balanced for me, perhaps isn't the same for you. This is why you should never seek the solution outside of yourself, but within yourself.

CAREER WOMAN

People often say that I work too much, but I disagree. I love my work! My work gives me so much creativity, and I love to create. But, of course, not every part of my business is enjoyable. For example, I find no gratification in administrative tasks, but developing strategy, planning, creating something new, writing articles or books and holding Beautyrobic trainings or webinars are all exciting, challenging jobs that I truly enjoy.

Since I know which parts of my job I enjoy most, I find balance by focusing more time and energy on the parts I enjoy. Work feeds my creative energy, which makes me feel more invigorated and energized when I leave work at the end of the day. I've not only found a job that I love, but I have found a way to end my workday on a high note. I never go home exhausted or wishing I didn't have to work so much. This is how I create balance in my workplace.

You can do the same in your own job by finding what areas energize you and what areas you love. If there are parts of your job you absolutely hate or drag you down, you can try coming at it from a different angle to restore balance. If you happen to be in a position where you can assign those tasks to someone else, or outsource the work, that is another way to look at relieving the stress and pressure from doing the things you don't like in your job.

Once you have found the perfect job, make sure that you don't overdo it in the long term. Make time for your other roles too. Focusing too much of your time on one role may lead to imbalance over time. This is especially true if you need to be strict and bossy in you work, or you need to "fight" with others for success. This aligns more with masculine energy, to the detriment of femininity. A solution to this situation that works for me is trying to delegate the tasks that require masculine energy. But if you don't have this option, another solution is to compensate with feminine energy activities that help you back to balance. I will expand more on these later.

MOTHER

It is very important for a child to grow up in a well-balanced, happy family where they spend quality time with their parents. In the first few months of a child's life, it is usually the mother who meets the baby's basic needs. The emotional health of the mother greatly affects the physical and emotional development of a baby.[70]

---

70 Kristen Rogers, "Depression and Anxiety During and After Pregnancy May Harm Childhood Development, Study Finds," CNN Health, September 15, 2020, https://www.cnn.com/2020/09/15/health/maternal-mental-health-childhood-development-wellness/index.html.

If the mother is relaxed and well-balanced, the baby will develop well both physically and emotionally. Conversely, if the mother is anxious and constantly nervous, eventually the baby will also develop these emotions. Therefore, it is very important, not only for your own wellbeing but also for the wellbeing of your child, that you try to find a good balance. Part of that balance includes self-care, plenty of rest and taking breaks as much as you can. Mothers can experience drastic changes in mood and hormones after giving birth. If these changes impact the mother's inner balance, mental health, and child's well-being, it is important to seek professional care to help restore that balance.

When you become a mother, you are no longer responsible for yourself but also for your children, which involves sacrifice. However, you still have needs that should be reflected in the way you arrange your life and how you balance your various roles. There is no ideal ratio that works for everyone; it must be specific to you.

PARTNER

When we talk about the role of a partner (i.e., wife, girlfriend, significant other, etc.), we need to examine it from two different perspectives. You need to have the right proportions in your various roles, but don't forget that you also need to create a **balance between partners** within your relationship. I see plenty of joyless, troubled relationships where partners don't lift each other up and instead negatively affect each other.

I interviewed Mihaela Nistor, a psychologist who specializes in relationships. She is a practicing psychologist and psychology professor, so is well versed in relationships. Mihaela mentioned something very interesting she heard at one of the lectures of Peter

Popper, who quoted Milán Füst.[71]

To achieve a harmonious relationship, there are four factors that must be balanced between partners. The lack of any one of these factors may lead to problems and disagreements. Mihaela agreed, from a psychological perspective, that these are foundational aspects that support the success of relationships.

4 FACTORS OF BALANCE IN A PARTNERSHIP

1. Love

2. Similar lifestyle

3. Sex

4. Similar financial situation

If these four factors are very different between two people, it is difficult to create harmony.

First of all, love and acceptance of each other are important, they are the basis of everything.

The next factor is similar lifestyle. It is necessary for couples to be able to spend quality time together. For example, if you hate beach vacations but that's all your partner wants to do, or you love going to the theater but he loves rock concerts, sooner or later it may cause problems between you. Just consider the arguments that may arise if you love dogs and can't live without them, but your

---

71 Krisztina, Germus. "Ha Felborul a Négylábú Asztal – Instabilitás A Kapcsolatokban." Mindset Pszichológia, November 23, 2018. https://mindsetpszichologia.hu/ha-felborul-a-negylabu-asztal-instabilitas-a-kapcsolatokban.

partner won't tolerate them in the house and hates the barking and pet hair! Even eating habits can cause problems. If you are health conscious, work out and maintain a very healthy lifestyle while your partner is a chain smoker who loves pizza and beer every night, regardless of whether you are madly in love, you may find yourselves extremely annoyed by each other. If two people have radically different lifestyles, sooner or later it will lead to alienation within the relationship.

Sex is another factor where different things can make each partner happy. This is perfectly fine! The problems arise when you and your partner have distinctly different sexual needs. The things that give us sexual pleasure may vary greatly from one individual to other, and if these desires don't match within a relationship, it may lead to problems over time.

Lastly, each individual's financial situation is important too. This does not mean that the level of happiness in the relationship depends on the exact amount of the money each of you has. What does matter is each partner's attitude towards money and spending habits. If one of you is always frugal and saving money while the other spends money like there's no tomorrow, that can become the source of arguments. Attitudes towards the role of money in our lives can also become a source of conflict. A radical difference between partners on this factor may lead to discord.

Of course, a harmonious relationship doesn't depend on these factors exclusively. It takes effort and work from both parties to create harmony, and establishing ideal male and female roles is extremely important.

It is also important to balance your relationship and the other roles in your life. You can find what balance is best for you, but you should always make time for yourself separate from your partner and have interests, friends and activities you do without them. This can extend to your role as a mother, in your career and your family as well. A partnership shouldn't occupy your entire life or limit your ability to have balance within your other roles, and it shouldn't take away from who you are as an individual or at your core.

LOVER

What I mean by a lover is not that you should be with someone in addition to your partner. This feminine role is focused on not losing the sexuality inside you and making it an essential part of your life. Sadly, many women tend to neglect this role, which may cause problems on both the physical and spiritual level. It can also have a negative effect on a woman's femininity. This is especially true for couples who have been married or have been partners for a long time. You and your partner should have a healthy, consistent sex life, based on both of your levels of interest and desire, which also explores each of your fantasies and sexual preferences. In some relationships, this kind of intimacy can fade over time. Keeping it alive is important to you as a woman as well as to your relationship.

Not having this balance may knock your partner role out of balance as well. You shouldn't neglect this because it is just as important as the others. You should listen to your innermost desires and feelings. Talk about them openly with your partner, and if you feel that for some reason it is still not in balance, try to find a solution to restore balance. In terms of attractiveness, sexual attractiveness is so important that I have dedicated a separate chapter to it, which you will find at the end of the book.

BALANCE YOUR FEMININE ENERGY

One more important thing about balance is balancing our feminine energy. Remember the definition of feminine energy from the beginning of the previous section? We often don't pay as much attention to it as we should, and that can stop you from feeling your charisma and true attractiveness. This can negatively impact your sexual allure when you want to encourage intimate relationships. Without this energy, it's easy to get stuck being a friend when you want to take the relationship further. It can also hinder your ability to succeed in the career world—if you're constantly trying to match men and their masculine energy in the workplace, you ignore the powers that you inherently have as a woman, powers that can make you just as successful, if not more, in the male-dominated workforce.

When it comes to attractiveness, feminine energy cannot be ignored. It isn't about looks or external beauty. It's an inner energy that's elusive, but powerful. It contributes strongly to your inner radiance and thus to your attractiveness and charisma. It is great because it is ageless. It is not related to the fact that you are 20, 40 or 60 years old. You can acquire it at any time with the right exercises.

A lady with one of the strongest feminine energies I have ever met was in Vienna, Austria. It was a short but astonishing experience that I'll remember forever.

Anyone who has ever been to Vienna's famous main street, Karntner Strasse, knows that there are lots of cafés in the middle of the street where you can sit out in the summer. It is very nice to walk there in good weather and enjoy the sun. The last time I was there, a woman was sitting on the terrace of one of the street cafés and as I looked up, she was lifting her coffee cup to her mouth. The movement, the way she sat, the way she held the cup in her hand and the way she lifted it to her mouth was so graceful. There was so much feminine energy in the whole act that I rarely see being expressed by other women. Even though she was simply dressed and did nothing unusual, her radiance was so strong that it was impossible not to look at her. There was so much special strength and feminine energy in that simple movement that no makeup or dress could compete with. I remember it was such a defining experience for me because I saw the incredible power of this type of energy and realized that it really needs to be addressed.

Nowadays, women need to do so many things that require masculine energy. Just think about fighting for some purpose, like for a promotion or job title or when we want to be successful at marketing ourselves. These tasks often require masculine energy in the form of aggression, ambition and determination. Women are practically forced to ignore their natural strengths to succeed in a man's world. That doesn't mean that women can't succeed with their own strengths; they just need to be reminded of them. After all, in the 21st century, women's roles have changed and what we have been fighting for so long has now finally become a reality in many parts of the world. On the other hand, there is now an even greater need to counterbalance this in our lives and pay conscious attention to strengthening our feminine energy so that there is a perfect balance in our lives.

In this section, I want to help you see how you can develop and increase this feminine energy within yourself so that you too can have a balance in this area.

Arts

Arts and creativity, like singing, dancing, literature, poems, drawing, coloring or cooking, or anything that relaxes you, recharges you or fills you with happiness develops your feminine energy. Female energy is about creation. Carrying a child under your heart is also a kind of creation. That's why everything related to creation will help you develop your femininity. Whether you love to cook, draw, garden or write a poem, do it, because it recharges you and increases your feminine energy too.

Dancing is also an art. I mentioned before that feminine, isolated movements during workouts like Beautyrobic or various dances classes (salsa, belly dance, bachata, etc.) are not only important because they benefit our figure and health, but because they help women to increase their feminine energy. So, don't be afraid to dance, feel the rhythm, sing and surrender yourself to different forms of arts.

Compensate

Be careful not to let life harden you. I'm not saying, of course, that you should leave your job if you're working in a position that requires you to be tough, but make sure you consciously compensate for that by doing exercises that harmonize your female energies.

I have a friend with a very spiritual mindset who has known me since I was 18. When I opened my own Beautyrobic Center in Budapest, I tried to pay attention to every detail. Not only did I hold classes, but I was also the site manager. I oversaw instructors and receptionists and kept the place tidy and everything going smoothly. Of course, there were problems that had to be solved and there were times when it was necessary for me to play the "bad cop." While I could do this if I needed to, I felt like it was making me harder and colder than I wanted to be. One day, I went into the center and a friend from my Beautyrobic class was waiting for me outside. She looked at me and asked what had happened to me because my energy was so unusual. I realized that because of this strict role, my female energy had begun to decline. I learned that it is better for me to stick to the owner role, doing the creative work, creating a strategy and holding Beautyrobic classes, because this is what I love. I gave the role of everyday manager to someone else. If you can't outsource your tasks like I did, don't despair, just be sure to compensate with the right amount of female energy-boosting activities to keep yourself in balance.

Look inside

It's great to set goals, but if you focus on goals alone, it can negatively affect your feminine energy. Going towards a goal without caring about anything develops masculine energy. I held a goal planning workshop at the beginning of one year where one of the participants, a very purposeful woman, was stuck in her life. She cared about herself and her career and was seemingly perfect, yet she couldn't get from A to B. What was wrong with her mindset was that her many goals, plans and tasks distracted her from her feelings and inner voice. My advice to her was not to do something, but quite the opposite. I asked her to give herself a few months where she didn't plan but just lived in the moment, paying attention to her inside and noting what she was feeling, what she really wanted, her intuitions and her feelings. The problem is not that you have goals. It's good to have goals. Later, I'll discuss how it can have a positive effect on attractiveness to have goals, but sometimes you must keep quiet and look inside, so you know where you're going and what you really want deep down in your heart.

Dealing with stress

What is your stress management strategy? If something worries you, how quickly can you overcome it? Do you have time to recharge and relax? A nervous wreck or an aggressive, tense woman can't be charismatic and full of feminine energy. Therefore, it's important to incorporate different stress management techniques into your life.

Taking walks in nature, listening to chirping birds, getting sunshine or walking barefoot on the grass are not only excellent stress relieving activities, but they fill you with so much energy that you will shine from afar. When I feel like I'm running out of energy, a great walk always helps me.

Meditate (and try our Meditattractiveness program)

I think one of the best techniques for harmonizing our energy levels is meditation. I have been meditating regularly for a long time and I love how I see things from a very different perspective afterwards. That's why, with the help of a psychologist, I created meditations specifically for developing femininity, as well as Meditattractiveness, which is specifically invented to harmonize and increase female energy.

Women's community

The development of female energy is like the development of intuition. If you listen to it, it gets stronger.

Admire the femininity and the feminine energy in other women and try to see the aura that surrounds them. Try to see this even in a simple gesture. You can learn a lot about feminine energy by joining a women's community or an activity like Beautyrobic. Being around other women who are empowered in their feminine energy is another way to connect to your own.

Develop a ritual and a routine that develops female attractiveness.

You become what your habits make you. If you want to be more feminine, then increase the number of feminine energy-boosting habits you do. Do Beautyrobic exercises daily, put on some sexy music and roll your hips. Meditate or do Meditattractiveness exercises. Beautyrobic has developed a lot of rituals that can be introduced into your everyday life. Here, I would like to share two of them with you as a gift.

Breathing ritual: Stand in the garden or on a balcony. If you've got neither or it's too cold then stand in front of a window, preferably when the sun is shining. Close your eyes and think about what you are grateful for in your life. Then take a deep breath, stretch up your arms high and stroke your face and body softly with your hands as you exhale. Then think of another reason you are grateful, and again, inhaling with your hands up high, exhale and stroke your body. Repeat this at least 5 times.

Shower ritual: When you take a shower, forget about traditional body cleaning and imagine yourself as if you were in an erotic shower scene in an 80s thriller. Pour your shower gel slowly into your palm and spread it on your whole body very sensually. Feel and enjoy the whole movement. Observe it with all your senses. Feel how the water touches your body, as the shower gel slides in your hand, enjoy its silkiness, the smell of it. Perhaps the best way to describe it is to take a shower like a goddess.

Awaken your sensuality

If you want to increase your female energy from within, one of the most important components is awakening and developing your sensuality. This is one of the many positive side effects that our Beautyrobic guests report. Or often, it's their partners or friends who are grateful for this effect. Developing sensuality is not like giving makeup advice, where I might show you how to do something and you can repeat it. It is a much longer process where you need practice and patience. But believe me, it's worth it.

As this topic is closely related to sexuality and I consider the experience of sexuality to be very important in relation to attractiveness, I have devoted a separate chapter to this topic (Chapter 7: Let's talk about sex...) where we will discuss this in more detail.

By now, you will see that achieving balance is more complex than it first seems, as there are so many aspects to consider. Attaining balance is not easy, and even if we have attained it once, there's no guarantee that we will remain in balance forever. It requires continuous work, self-reflection and self-examination. Always pay attention to your inner signals because they will caution you whenever you are not in balance. You will feel it deep down when something is not right or is not what you truly desire. We are all different and our needs and desires are different too. To be balanced, you need to know what it is that you want, your deepest desires, and for that you will need conscious awareness.

A FOR AWARENESS

The second part of the B.A.G. level is awareness. How is awareness connected to attractiveness?

If you are aware of who you are, and know your strengths, weaknesses, values and worth, you will have a special sparkle around you that people will find attractive. You will be able to express who you really are, and people will understand it, so you will attract the right people to you.

Those who are lost and do not know what they want in life live their life without awareness. Often, they let others tell them what they should do because they don't want to take responsibility for their life. If they don't know who they are, how can others know?

The first step involves you consciously getting to know yourself. Who are you and what do you really want? Don't think of gigantic things. Becoming a star or being famous is not the objective here. Fame or chasing fame sidetracks a whole lot of people. I often see young girls and women chasing a daydream that is not their real path.-

Get to know your path and be attentive to your signals. Make note of the things you like and what you don't like. Pay attention to who and what makes you feel fulfilled. Remember, a large part of life consists of the journey and not the destination. The destination is worthless if you hate the journey that leads up to it. Whatever your goal may be, the journey has multiple paths and you will need to choose the right path for you—the one that you enjoy and can feel balanced in!

HOW TO FIND THE RIGHT PATH FOR YOUR GOALS

OBSERVE YOUR THOUGHTS AND FEELINGS CONSCIOUSLY!

Observe how a given situation or event affects you. What feelings does it evoke? What natural reaction does it trigger in you? If something depletes you, and you feel that no matter what you do or how hard you keep trying, it will never work, the chances are that you are on the wrong path.

Let me give you a simple example. If your goal is to lose weight and become physically fit, there are various ways to achieve that goal. Your task is to find the method that is appropriate for you. Find a sport you truly love doing and stick to a diet you can incorporate into your everyday life and matches your taste. There may be a super effective diet that involves eating lots of meat, but it is the wrong method for you if you hate meat.

There's a woman who attends my Beautyrobic classes regularly. One day, she told me that this was the first exercise routine she really enjoys doing, which is why she has managed to stick to exercising regularly. So, it's no wonder that with this program, she has managed to achieve the results she wanted. After innumerable failed attempts, she has managed to lose weight with a method that she truly enjoys! Sometimes you have the right goal, but the wrong method.

So, please do not stick to a method you are failing in. Many other paths exist to reach the same goal; you just need to choose the one that fits you. Failure is a moment to learn, grow and change. Be aware of what worked or didn't work and why, then try again with a more appropriate method.

Let me give you another example. If you want to become successful, there is more than one way to do it. You can become an influencer who is followed by millions, but if you hate posting on social media, this is not your path to success. You can come up with a good idea for how to help people solve a problem and build a business around it, or you can learn finance and start investing, or you can work hard in your current workplace to be promoted. I want you to realize that there is not only one way to reach your goals. You need to find the path that's the right fit for you and will make you happy. This is important.

YOU NEED TO RECOGNIZE WHAT IT IS YOU REALLY WANT!

It is *you* who, by your extraordinary alchemy, can transform a profession into something special and interesting. It's not being a model or an actor that will make someone attractive. What makes someone attractive is that they are successful at what they do.

Elon Musk, Sara Blakely, Oprah Winfrey and even the woman who makes the best pancakes in the neighborhood all exude charm and magnetism. What is your special talent? Where do you add value and where do you excel? That's what you need to find. Only then will you have an unceasing feeling of accomplishment, and people will admire you for it.

What is a calling that you could enjoy doing every day? Here, I deliberately avoided the word "job" and used "calling" instead, because there is a dramatic difference between the two! A job is what people do because they have to, while one's calling is usually what they would do even if they won the lottery and could afford to quit. One's calling is not driven by money but is a mission. I would define a calling as your life's purpose or passion.

A calling has telltale signs. You will know it because, once you have found it, you will feel alive inside. You will feel enthusiasm, learn much faster and find that the process itself enjoyable. Once we discover our calling, suddenly, we find meaning in life. Your calling won't necessarily be something grandiose or world-changing, but you will feel fulfilled and happy doing it. Don't be distracted by society, advertisements or other people's expectations. Look inwards to find what it is you really want!

How can you discover this? Ask yourself the following questions and respond to them in writing— truthfully and sincerely!

EXERCISE

Think about these questions and then respond to them honestly. **Don't read on until you have completed them!**

- What makes you truly happy?

- What do you do that makes other people happy?

- What do you consider the most important thing in your life?

- Do you genuinely love what you are doing, or are you doing it for the singular purpose of earning the money necessary to support yourself or your family?

- What is the skill that people praise you for? What is something you do very well or better than average? (Think of the simple things, too!)

- When was the last time you had a good laugh? What makes you laugh? How could you laugh more/be happier?

- How far away do you think you are from the things you want to achieve? What would you need to do to achieve them? What's blocking you from doing it?

- What can you do right now to move closer to your goals?

- What are you going to do to reach your goals in the next month, year and five years?

There's no rush. Stop for a quiet moment. Sit down and take your time to deeply think about these answers!

Trust me, it's worth taking the time to go through these questions, because when you find what you really want, you will find your reason to get up every morning. You will not only be happy, but you will have an inexplicable sparkle and fire inside you that will attract other people to you like a magnet!

WARNING!

You should know that even though you have found your path, it will still take dedication, willpower and perseverance to reach your goals! You can't spare yourself from the work if you want to achieve results. Talent alone will get you nowhere if you don't pair it with hard work! The world is filled with talented but lazy people who have achieved little in their lives because they relied on their talent alone and refused to put in the work. Don't be one of them!

EXERCISE

Consider the following questions with regards to your romantic and other personal relationships:

- Who do you want to surround yourself with? What kind of friends do you want?

- What are the characteristics you would like the partner of your dreams to have?

- What does your ideal future family look like?

- What does your current situation look like compared to these ideals?

- What would you need to do to achieve your dream? What's blocking you from doing it? What can you do right now to get one step closer to it?

- What are you going to do to achieve your goals in the next month, year and five years?

Give yourself time and think over your answers to these questions! When you reflect on them, please consider the below paragraph.

EVERYTHING HAS A PRICE!

Everybody wants to be happy, rich, popular, good-looking, intelligent and admired in life. If you ask someone what they long for, you can bet that they will mention one or more of these factors, or perhaps all of them. It is perfectly understandable. Who wouldn't want to achieve any of those goals? But people don't want to recognize that everything has a price in life, and that price must be paid whether one likes it or not.

If you want to be fit, you must go to the gym and work out, either before work early in the morning or after working hours when you would rather get some rest. If you are a stay-at-home mum with a child around, you must exercise even when you are exhausted and would rather wrap yourself in a fuzzy blanket and go to bed. On top of that, you must also pay attention to your diet, and you can't always eat what you crave. You must practice self-control at every family gathering and in every store or restaurant.

Do you want a great career, leadership position or generous salary, but don't really want to put in all that overtime, study or dedicate your weekends and evenings to trainings and work? Do you want to become popular or famous, but would rather not deal with constant rejection? Could you put up with all that unpredictability, lack of money and unpaid work until you are discovered? That could happen for 10 years, or forever.

Do you want to become a wealthy entrepreneur? Are you prepared to take risks in life? Do you want to spend your salary on something that could be hit or miss? Do you want to dedicate your free time to something that won't bring in money right away, and may even cost money, while working full time during the day? Do you want a second job beside the one you have? Do you want to juggle your potential clients on the weekends and in the evenings?

Ultimately, the question is not, "What do I want?" but, "What am I willing to tolerate?" This is the way life goes. If you want to get something, sooner or later you will have to pay the price! Do you want a fit body? Great! Who wouldn't want one? But how do you deal with the road that leads there? Some people can endure the "suffering" of getting up two hours earlier every morning to go to the gym or using their free time to go to Beautyrobic classes or another workout. Some people are conscious of their diet and frequently dedicate extra time to preparing food that's good for them. Those are the people who have truly amazing bodies.

You shouldn't aspire to the result alone! You need to weather the road that leads there and embrace it. The road maybe long, but it will lead you where you want to go. One of the most critical steps on the bumpy road to self-awareness is learning to be honest with yourself. In other words, you need to sincerely reflect on both your strengths and weaknesses. Do you really want that goal enough to pay its price? Of course, most of us would like to imagine ourselves as a Hollywood celebrity, but many of today's famous actors had to endure years and years of rejection, hardships, hunger and poverty. Would you be willing to pay that price?

Remember, in life everything has a price. That's the way life goes!

I cannot stress enough that you must find your own path, because in the long run, you can only put energy into something that you have a true passion for! That is why there is no one-size-fits-all solution to reach your goals! There are roughly 7 billion people in the world, and no one is just like you. We are all different! We have different dreams, potential and talents. This is also why only you can know what's best for you and what makes you happy. Even someone who means well and has good intentions will not necessarily give you good advice! So, we shouldn't always listen to others. Especially if what they say contradicts your own intuition. Believe me, if you are on the right track, you will feel it without a doubt. You will also feel it when you are on the wrong track.

TAKE RESPONSIBILITY

You must learn to make decisions and assume responsibility for them and for your life. Remember, if your current situation doesn't serve you, it is your responsibility to do what it takes to change it. Even if your circumstances are not your fault, it is still your responsibility to do something to change it! Improve your life, become happier and fix what you feel isn't working. Often, people don't act because they are busy finding blame with someone else. They limit themselves by repeatedly deflecting blame and stopping themselves from finding the solution. Instead, they choose to agonize over the problem. Perhaps the initial problem wasn't your fault, but the fact it isn't your fault doesn't mean it isn't your responsibility to fix it.

Let me illustrate this with a few examples.

It is not your fault if your parents could not afford your education and had no chance to provide you with opportunities, but it is your responsibility to take control of your destiny as an adult and do everything you can to live the life of your dreams. Once, a woman approached me after a Beautyrobic class and told me how lucky I was that things were easy for me because I was successful and well connected, whereas she had a messed-up family and negative friends. I asked her how old she was and she said she was about to turn 30. I told her that the things she had told me about her life could be considered valid excuses until she turned 18 years old, but from that point on, she needed to take responsibility to her life. She thought I was just lucky, but the truth is, it was not luck. I grew up in modest circumstances and my parents couldn't afford my university fees, or give me money to start my businesses or even for me to have fun with classmates after school. But I did not blame them for it, and I know they tried their best. When I was 16, I looked for a part-time job after school and studied harder so I could have a chance to win a scholarship at my chosen university. During secondary school, I would hold workout classes at a gym, while going to school and preparing myself for my AP, SAT and university entrance exams. Even though I couldn't control what opportunities my parents could provide, I worked hard to give myself those opportunities another way.

So, let's quit looking for excuses and blaming others! Let's focus on finding solutions instead! Life gives different opportunities and problems to each of us, but we can't get the most out of everything until we realize that the capability to change is in our hands. If we take responsibility and start working on solutions, we can win. Especially nowadays, thanks to the Internet, we have so many opportunities to change our life for the better, even without any money or a strong financial background. Let's not resign ourselves to our fate but be in control of our own destiny. Let's act!

THE BOILING FROG

I find that people often fall more and more into a routine as they get older and subsequently get further and further from the life they really wish to live. They accept the hand that they have been dealt, even if it's not at all what they wanted. They resign themselves to their destiny and circumstances, or perhaps they don't even realize how far they have drifted away from their deepest desires. This phenomenon is very similar to the "boiling frog" syndrome. If a frog is dropped in boiling water suddenly, it will immediately spring out of it. It finds the heat unbearable and wants to change its circumstances. However, if the same frog is dropped in cold water that is then brought to boil gradually, it can be cooked without it resisting. The reason is that the frog doesn't perceive the gradual change in the temperature of the water. A similar phenomenon is frequently experienced by people, too.

If something worsens gradually, people don't tend to fight against it. They fail to perceive the estrangement of their romantic relationship or the detachment of their marriage, they become accustomed to the increasing monotony of their jobs and don't perceive the growing number of conflicts with their colleagues as a problem. Slowly but surely, they get further and further from the life they desire deep in their hearts. They don't even perceive the change because it doesn't happen overnight. They imagine a life for themselves, but then they compromise their dream in one area, then in another, and another, until their life is nowhere near the one they had in mind.

This is often the case with weight gain. Many people are fit in their 20s, but begin to put on a few pounds every year, and over time, they accept those 45 extra pounds because the negative change has occurred gradually.

LUKEWARM LIFE

The other struggle people get stuck in is what I call the "lukewarm life" effect. What exactly do I mean by that? A lukewarm life is a negative situation that is not what you wanted it to be but is not bad enough to make you change it. If there's one thing that can make your life miserable, it is the lukewarm water effect. It's a romantic relationship that is not bad enough to make you leave, so you settle, or a workplace you hate going to, but could be worse, so you stay. It could be a body which is not too bad, and some people have worse-looking bodies, so it will do. Or a trip that is not the vacation of your dreams, but at least you get to go somewhere. It is a state when you are living your life in a way that is far from dreamlike but is at least bearable. The lukewarm water effect is when things that are not bad enough to get fed up and say, "Enough of this!"

What happens when something is outright unbearable? You

spring into action immediately and fight against it. There's always a breaking point, a point where you finally stand up and say, "I can't take it anymore!" It is when you reach the point where anything else seems better than the situation you are in that you take action to improve it.

But these moments are rare. What we experience most of the time is a basic, tolerable life, where it is more comfortable for us to be stuck than to act. Why? For a very simple reason. It's not easy to step out of your comfort zone. It's not easy to go to the gym regularly before or after work, or say no to cake, or learn something new, acquire new skills or start all over again. Stepping out of your comfort zone to make radical changes is hard and intimidating, and since it is different from what is normal and ordinary, it makes us feel insecure. So, rather than push through the discomfort, we remain stuck in our ordinary, lukewarm lives!

What happens if you choose comfort? Things will continue to be the way they've always been—not bad, but not good either! That is what I call the lukewarm water effect. I'm begging you to not settle for a lukewarm life! Don't be afraid to change the things you don't like. It's never too late!

I talked earlier about fear and overcoming fear. Make sure you complete the exercises aimed at overcoming fear, because you deserve to live the life of your dreams! Don't deceive yourself! If you are not in balance with your life right now, it will not change if you keep doing everything the same way you always have. People often expect different results while they repeat the same actions over and over. If you want something different, then you must change, and your life will change with you!

Do not turn away from hardship but confront your problems as they occur. Often, we find the solution to our problems when we take the time to write them down in detail and explain their root cause. You need to regulate and check in on yourself constantly. You need to exercise continuous self-control so that you can lead your life in a truly conscious way. Being conscious of your life means that you know who you are, what you want and what direction you are heading. This will give you a certain confidence in yourself that will make you extremely attractive to others around you.

G FOR GROWTH

Think of life being like a Lego construction set. There is a huge bucket full of all kinds of bricks, gears and various parts. The Lego pieces are the various possibilities and opportunities in your life.

What school will you attend? What will you study? Where will you live? Where will you work? What kind of partner will you choose? What kind of people will you be surrounded by? It's up to you to pick out the pieces you would like to have, the ones that appeal to you the most, and to use them creatively to build a wonderful life for yourself. If you fail to select your own pieces, someone else will pick the pieces for you, and it's likely that you wouldn't have selected the same pieces for yourself.

You must make your own life decisions. You need to build your life, develop and improve. Those who sit idly by and do nothing to improve their own life will stop growing as a person. Dare to dream big! Don't let society, co-workers, friends, family or anyone else influence you. It is your life and your Lego castle!

And how is this connected to attractiveness? Why is growth involved in the B.A.G. level?

Those who want to grow, who have goals in their life that they work on every day, even when it is difficult, have a special sparkle. They have a fire in their eyes that makes them so attractive that people cannot resist them. Life with them is never boring because they are constantly progressing and become better, day by day. It is so charismatic when somebody is intelligent and able to talk about anything. It is magnetic when someone becomes better and better in their field and you can feel their passion about their chosen topic. These people are attractive and others enjoy being close to them.

From the moment I understood what I really wanted, I no longer cared about what other people expected of me. I focused my attention on what I thought was the right thing, what made me happy and what I identified with. Immediately, I was filled with a liberating feeling, the freedom of self-acceptance and self-confidence. Being true to myself liberated me and made me very attractive to others! The air about you when you can express yourself, your visions and what you really want is the only secret to becoming naturally attractive. There's no artificial, make-believe perfection that could ever match that!

Devote time to self-awareness and growth. Use baby steps to gradually build the Lego castle of your life! Plan out everything! When we discussed awareness, I elaborated on why it is critical that we know who we are and what we want. At this level, our task is working towards putting this into practice.

There is only one secret to achieving big dreams and goals: Split them up to smaller tasks and subgoals

Of course, the more ambitious the goal, the longer it'll take you to achieve it. But that doesn't make it impossible! Many people get scared of big, ambitious dreams or goals, and out of fear, lower their expectations. Your dreams die when fear gets in the way. This is tragic, because even the biggest goals are attainable in small steps!

Think of reaching your goals as a journey. Decide where you want to travel, and then plan out the steps to get there. It is possible to get to the other side of the world, it will just take more steps and extra time. You must know where you want to arrive, and then act accordingly. Take your big goals, plan out the steps, identify the tools you need, set a deadline, and develop a strategy to achieve it. Only with a plan and perseverance will it become attainable.

Let's take losing weight as an example. Let's say you want to lose 90 pounds, which may seem unattainable all at once, but if you divide it into subgoals, it will be much less intimidating. For example, losing one pound per week by giving up sugar or carbs and taking Beautyrobic classes three times a week. Your goal will feel much more attainable like this.

EXERCISE

Work out a strategy for the goals you developed from your answers to the questions in the awareness section. Split them up into subgoals, assign tasks to each subgoal, and designate the tools you will need for the execution of these tasks. Set a deadline to achieving them!

INCREASING PRODUCTIVITY WITH TIME MANAGEMENT

Everyone has 24 hours in a day, but not everyone is able to use them with the same efficiency. Some people hardly accomplish anything, while others manage to cram so much into one day it's as if five people were working simultaneously. Many people claim that the reason they don't work out or look after themselves is that they don't have time. Yet, there are many women who make time for themselves despite having kids and a career to juggle! I believe that everything is a question of how much determination you have. Let's not look for excuses, but rather for solutions.

I talked to a friend of mine who works on Wall Street in New York City. It's common knowledge that those on Wall Street work extremely hard. I asked him how he manages to be so efficient. He works as a commercial director and is responsible for the entire East Coast of the U.S. and Canada, yet he still manages to make time outside of work to exercise regularly, have fun with friends and even date. He said his secret is that he divides his tasks into 30-minute increments, and by doing so, he can productively accomplish everything each day. Everybody can focus on one task for 30 minutes, and then it doesn't seem so long and never-ending.

A study from Kansas State University determined that one of the best ways to maximize productivity and focus is to stick to one subject, topic or task for 30–45 minutes.[72] The study recommends setting timers to remind you when the 30–45 minutes is up and it is time to focus on something else. This allows you to focus solely

---

72 "Here's Why You Should Only Study for 30 Minute Stretches (Plus 9 More Tips)," The Nook, March 27, 2019, https://www.crown.edu/nook/heres-why-you-should-only-study-for-30-minute-stretches-plus-9-more-tips/.

on one task or topic for a designated time frame, without worrying that you won't have time to do more. It can be applied to work, but also in your personal life, hobbies and relationships.[73]

EXERCISE

Put your daily tasks on a to-do list and try to accomplish them in 30-minute chunks! Make sure you do something every day to increase your own attractiveness! Schedule some of the magnetism-maximizing tasks in this book every day.

PLANNING IS NOT ENOUGH, WE MUST ACT!

There are some people who are all talk and no action. They are good at planning but unfortunately, that's not enough. The problem lies in their attitude, because they approach everything without putting in either the energy or the work! Regardless of planning, when that is not paired with action, you will not see any results.

Whether it's concerning romantic relationships, your career or other human connections, it takes a lot of energy, work and an all-out effort! If you want to obtain spectacular results in any area of your life, then take action and put in 110% effort. If you want to stand out from others, put this into practice. Adopting the right

---

73 Ibid.

attitude is critical. Make it a habit that when you do something, you always put in 110% effort to make sure you do it well.

BE EFFICIENT!

A lot of people are diligent and go to great lengths, but still can't get ahead. Rather than doing more, do it better and in a way that's relevant to the goal!

If you go to the gym for a workout, how thorough those exercises are makes a huge difference to whether they serve your intended purpose or not!

Twenty-four hours a day is not much, so when we compile our to-do list, we must carefully weigh all the factors!

Here is some help on what to consider when you compile your to-do list:

Does this new task help me to achieve my goals (including the long-term ones)?

Is it necessary that I do the job personally, or could someone else do it just a well, and allow me to dedicate my time to much more useful and important things in the meantime?

Do I enjoy doing it or not? Is the only reason I've got to do this is to not hurt someone else by rejecting his or her request?

LEARN TO SAY NO!

No matter how hard it is, you must learn to say no if you want to get the life you want! My husband used to say yes whenever people asked him favors. He didn't want to hurt people by rejecting their requests. Often, he ended up not making progress on his own tasks as a result, and he didn't perform the favors at the desired level either because he had too much to do. Although he did it with the best intentions, people were still mad at him in the end.

After a while, when I saw him struggle with this regularly, I suggested he learn to say no. After all, no one in their right mind would get mad at him if he responds to their requests with, "I'm sorry, but I can't help you with this one." This is better than the alternative of him saying yes, someone counting on him, and then later not delivering as expected.

Psychologist Pamela Mendelsohn says that saying no is a good practice for setting boundaries and shows respect.[74] When you say yes to someone and don't really want to, that can lead to resentment and create friction in the relationship over time. Saying no when you want to shows them that you can be honest and authentic. When you say no to one thing, you'll be allowed to say yes to something else. Saying no doesn't mean you are missing out, it means you are opening up different opportunities, ones you might like better.[75]

FINISH WHAT YOU START!

A lot of people have the enthusiasm to start something, but they

---

74 Pamela Mendelsohn, "The Importance of Saying 'No'," My Therapy NYC, July 26, 2019, https://mytherapynyc.com/importance-of-saying-no/.
75 Ibid.

are not strong enough to finish. The problem is that in the end they are no different to those who never started a task to begin with. It's like starting to run a marathon but stopping and giving up before the finish line. The result is the same; you haven't run a marathon.

If you create a profile on a dating app, but you don't respond to the messages you receive, it was all for nothing. If you subscribe to the Beautyrobic home program, but you don't use it to exercise, it's as if nothing happened, except that you have wasted away your energy and money with no result! There are so many people who dive into everything, but never finish anything. Don't be one of them! Resolve to start doing fewer things, but to finish everything that you commit to.

VISUALIZE WHAT YOU WANT!

"Whatever the mind can conceive and believe, it can achieve."
—Napoleon Hill[76]

Imagine in exact, meticulous detail what you desire—your goals, ambitions and the qualities you want to have. Close your eyes and picture yourself as the charismatic, radiant girl who sweeps people off their feet!

This is extremely important. When you visualize every day what you want to achieve, your brain will believe it to be true and grow increasingly more confident that you can make it a reality.

---

76 Napoleon Hill, *Think and Grow Rich* (New York: TarcherPerigee, Revised 2005).

You make yourself believe that it is an attainable, achievable goal! Often, we stand in the way of our own goals by subconsciously convincing ourselves that it's impossible to reach those goals and therefore we don't even try to achieve them!

I have a wall in my apartment where I display all my goals on a vision board, and I also put posters up of our wish-list travel destinations. When he gets up in the morning, my husband starts his day by writing down his goals and desires. I also have a friend who has her own vision board taped up on her fridge door. We do these things because they help us bring our goals and desires into sharper and stronger focus.

The morning is a great time of day to look at your goals or write down your affirmations. Our brain is very receptive at this time of day. You should begin your day with something useful, and even more importantly, something uplifting. When you get up in the morning, the first thing you think about after getting up is what will determine the trajectory of your whole day—and consequently your whole life!

THE THREE Ls
• LIFE LONG LEARNING •

Learn and improve! Whenever you get in a rut and don't know what to do, the solution should be to begin working on yourself! You should always start with yourself. If you don't know how to eat healthy or meal-plan, then start increasing your knowledge of nutrition. If you don't know how to dress with style, then start to educate yourself on fashion! If you feel like you are constantly trying to do something but not seeing any results, then it's time to broaden your horizon, expand your knowledge and begin developing yourself! Whenever I feel stuck in a rut, I always go back to studying and self-development. Life-long learning is the foundation of personal development. To grow, you need to develop yourself and your skills.

Why exactly is this important for our attractiveness? Because people always need new stimuli! The woman who can remain exciting in the long term is the one who has a capacity for transformation. If you want people to be attracted to you, seek and enjoy your company, choose you and stay with you for the long run, you will need to surprise them, electrify them and leave them open-mouthed. You need to be able to renew and become a better version of yourself! A person who ceases to improve is actually regressing. But the woman who has goals and aspirations has found her "why" in life, wants to progress, changes continually and grows in a positive direction. She will not only have that spellbinding fire in her eyes, but will also earn people's admiration and respect! She will never be boring.

FIND A MENTOR!

You don't have to go through this journey alone. If you feel like you need guidance, find a mentor who will help. Look for a person who inspires you! Everybody needs feedback in their lives.

You will have more strength to carry on and achieve your goals if there is someone who stands by to encourage you throughout the whole process. Everyone needs help and encouragement sometimes. Just think of the coaches of professional athletes who continuously support, motivate and strive to improve them. Or think about an app that shows you where you are, how far you've gone, whether your performance is mediocre or excellent and offers you encouragement to help propel you.

I believe that this has played a very important part in my success. When I get stuck, I have the courage to ask for input from other people or request help. I have always had someone to stand by and encourage me. If you feel you don't have a person in your life that does this, find yourself one or more mentors who are at a level you aspire to be at yourself who can help you solve issues as they arise.

chapter six

LEVEL V: INSPIRATION

READY, SET, INSPIRE!

There is a level of attractiveness that is ageless. It doesn't depend on outward appearance and is exactly how you can exert the most powerful level of attraction on others. Through this level, you will attract the people who are just right for you, like a giant magnet! This level is all about inspiring others. The likes of Oprah Winfrey, Adele, Barack Obama, Ed Sheeran and Tony Robbins inspire millions of people every day.

While the previous level was about personal development and finding balance within yourself, this level is about how to use your own personality, values and positivity to inspire others to be happier and feel more complete.

Inspire (verb) means the following:

> To make someone feel that they want to do something and can do it; To make someone have a particular strong feeling or reaction; To give someone an idea for a book, movie, product, etc.; To fill someone with confidence and desire to do something.

> Inspiring others is triggering something from within them. In other words, elevating them and supporting them in becoming more than who they have previously been.[77]

WHY IS THIS THE HIGHEST LEVEL OF ATTRACTIVENESS?

One of the most important people in your life is yourself. This is the longest relationship each of us will have in our lives. From our birth to our death, 24-7! If we find a person who helps us grow or become better, we want to be close to them and follow them to ensure that they are going to be a part of our lives.

What if you can have a positive effect on another person? What if through your unique qualities you can make someone feel more complete or happier? When you can become a positive influence in someone's life, they will become a better person as a result. People will seek out your company and will want to be near you, because through *you*, they become **more accomplished, more likeable and happier! This is the real power of inspiring others!**

---

77 "Inspire," Cambridge English Dictionary, accessed June 7, 2022, https://dictionary.cambridge.org/us/dictionary/english/inspire.

HOW CAN YOU TRULY INSPIRE OTHERS?

Oprah Winfrey said that inspiration is the "truest, highest expression of yourself."[78]

There are several ways that you can inspire others, but the one I want to teach you is how to inspire others with your true self. Don't be afraid to show who you really are! When you can live passionately and do what you believe in, showing your true self and your true "why," it will inspire other people. People will not remember the words you say, but the *way* you say them. It will be your passion, faith, and "why" that will truly inspire others.

To inspire others as your true self, you will need to complete the levels we discussed in the previous chapter. You need to know who you are, what your values are, what you love, and what you can do with your passion. You will also need to continually develop yourself. This is how you will be able to give to others, without crumbling under the pressure. You will need to be authentic and true to yourself.

The more you give to others, the more people you elevate, the more attractive you will become. Your charisma will be so strong that you will attract people like a magnet! The best part about it is that you will only attract people into your world who like you for who you really are. It will be your personality and uniqueness that will captivate them. They will appreciate the woman and the individual you are.

---

78 "5 Oprah Quotes from 2020 vision Tour LA," Fred Far, accessed June 7, 2022, https://fredandfar.com/blogs/ff-blog/5-oprah-quotes-from-2020-vision-tour-la.

What matters isn't how many people love you, or how many people seek your company, but whether those people respect and love you for who you are.

The number of people you can inspire largely depends on the magnitude of the channel you manage to build for your message and the values you are transmitting to them. You don't necessarily have to influence millions of people if that's not your aspiration. It can be just one person—a stranger, friend, or partner! It all depends on you and what you aspire to.

Believe me, there is nothing better than knocking people off their feet and inspiring them by being yourself and sharing your values. This is why the fourth level of L.o.R.A., B.A.G., is so important! To be able to give, first you need to get to know yourself. Everyone is talented, but many people are clueless about where their talents lie.

I hope that after having read the B.A.G. level, you already know what you want, but if you still have doubts, let me give you a hand!

We have all heard the word "intelligence," but most people think that only scientists or distinguished scholars can be truly intelligent. If we took a scientist and dropped them in a completely different job, for example in a theater, a bank or even in a gym, chances are that they would be a bit confused. There are several forms of intelligence, each depending on the way our brains function. It was Howard Gardner, a psychologist from Harvard

University, who developed the theory of multiple intelligences and published it in 1983, outlining the nine ways in which we can distinguish the major types of intelligence.[79] Although this theory has since been developed, it still is an excellent basis for finding your talent area.

By discovering where your intellectual strengths and aptitudes are, you can better understand where your talents lie and how they can be applied to your life and interests. It all comes back to knowing yourself and your strengths.

THE THEORY OF MULTIPLE INTELLIGENCES[80]

• READ IT THROUGH AND THINK IT OVER •

1. Linguistic-Verbal Intelligence

   The focus of this type of intelligence is verbal abilities. People with linguistic intelligence display a remarkable ability to express their thoughts and ideas through language. Bloggers, poets, rhetoricians, public speakers and communication experts are known for this type of

79 Kendra Cherry, "Gardner's Theory of Multiple Intelligences," Verywell Mind, July 28, 2021, https://www.verywellmind.com/gardners-theory-of-multiple-intelligences-2795161.

80 "Howard Gardner's Theory of Multiple Intelligences," Northern Illinois University, accessed June 7, 2022, https://www.niu.edu/citl/resources/guides/instructional-guide/gardners-theory-of-multiple-intelligences.shtml.

intelligence.

2. Logical-Mathematical Intelligence

We talk about logical–mathematical intelligence when people possess the ability to think analytically and recognize certain patterns, whether those are logical or numerical. People with this type of intelligence enjoy analyzing situations based on logic. This type of intelligence is often seen in scientists, mathematicians and detectives.

3. Visual-Spatial Intelligence

If you think using images and pictures, you probably possess spatial intelligence. The main characteristic of people with this type of intelligence is the ability to visualize problems. Artists, painters and architects are gifted with this type of intelligence.

4. Bodily-Kinesthetic Intelligence

This type of intelligence is when people can direct their body movements efficiently and with agility. Normally athletes, medical doctors and construction workers possess this kind of intelligence. Not surprisingly, every one of our Beautyrobic instructors possesses this type of intelligence.

5. Musical Intelligence

People with musical intelligence have a natural ability to create music and rhythm with ease. Musicians, singers, composers and DJs belong to this group.

6. Interpersonal Intelligence

   Interpersonal intelligence could be described as empathy, since essentially it is the ability to understand others. People with interpersonal intelligence are gifted in recognizing other people's emotions, desires and motivation. Caretakers, social workers, actors, politicians and teachers have this type of intelligence.

7. Intrapersonal Intelligence

   People with intrapersonal intelligence are interested in recognizing and understanding their own feelings. It is important for them to be in harmony with their own thoughts and to understand their own actions. Psychologists, writers and philosophers belong to this group.

8. Naturalistic Intelligence

   This type of intelligence evaluates and determines everything that comes from nature. People with this type of intelligence understand the laws of nature and make sense of them. Biologists, farmers, gardeners, chefs and hunters possess this talent.

9. Existential Intelligence

   Existential intelligence is found in people who reflect on the big questions in life, questioning the world, our existence and everything else. People who possess this kind of intelligence are mainly philosophers.

If you reflect on the list above, perhaps you will be able to identify which category you fall into. This can lead you to your passions, wants and talents in life, which will help you create value for other people and the world! Find what you can contribute to make the world a better place and elevate the lives of the people who matter to you. Don't be afraid to show your true self. Share with others, so that life can be elevated through you. There's no need to push yourself on others; you only need to learn to express who you truly are, and the people you motivate, touch and inspire will find you themselves. I emphasize this because I had to learn this in my life as well.

There was a time when it hurt and saddened me when someone wasn't receptive to what I expressed to them. Not because they didn't pay attention to me, but because I couldn't make them understand why my words were important. I just couldn't get over why they didn't understand that I was saying or doing something for their own good. Today, I know that I must let go of this. Not everyone is ready to grow, and you can't inspire everyone. They must decide for themselves. All you can do is offer them a possibility.

When you show other people the magic inside you, you will find you are surrounded with people who appreciate you. The man you want to sweep off his feet will be drawn to you and will see that you are different and special. A man you touch and inspire deeply won't have eyes for any other woman, regardless of looks or intelligence, because that other person will always have one fault: they are not *you*!

The partner you inspire will feel they become more fulfilled, happier and more successful through knowing you, so they would never trade you for anyone else in the world. You will be the fuel that keeps them moving.

Many people focus on quantity and want to capture the attention of as many people as possible. They emulate others because they think they will become more desirable and attractive that way. But when others admire you for something you are not, sooner or later they will find out and the delusion will end. This has happened to most people at one point in time or another. You meet someone in person for the first time after having formed an impression of them from pictures or on social media, but when you met them, they are totally different from how you imagined.

We have all heard stories about beloved actors who are seen by their fans as heroes because of their films, but in real life are conceited buffoons who are prone to hysterical outbursts. I know a girl who epitomizes the ideal woman in her Instagram photos— sophisticated, beautiful, elegant and reserved. But whenever I've introduced her to anyone, it has been a disaster. In real life, she is completely different from what her photos suggest. She is loud and over-the-top, which isn't necessarily a bad thing, but is completely different from what she portrays online!

If you really act like yourself, your *true* self, you will inspire the right people for you and will show your Real Attractiveness. Don't make the mistake of faking something only to make more people like or accept you. Pleasing everyone is impossible!

When you go on a date, just be yourself! If the man you had your eye on does not call you, he was not the right one for you. Be glad you found out early. If you pretend to be someone else just because you believe that it will make you more charismatic to a man, in the end you will realize that he doesn't like you or has fallen for a false version of you. In the long run, you won't be able to continue to pretend that you are someone else and at least one of the parties will be left very disappointed.

Why would you behave differently from how you really are? Why do you believe that who you truly are isn't good enough to be worthy of love?

If you put on a mask and aren't truly yourself, people will find out sooner or later! People will sense that you are forcing yourself to live up to the disingenuous image you have created. That will ultimately make you completely insecure!

This same thing applies to friends and coworkers. You want to fill your social circle with people that like you for you. You want friends who understand and support you. If you make friends based on a false persona, you'll find those friendships less fulfilling because they won't meet your actual needs.

In the workplace, when you are your genuine, true self, you will inspire your coworkers to be themselves too. When you're an individual and focused on your talents and strengths, you'll stand out in the workplace. When you try to emulate others, you'll become just another cog in the machine that won't ever be noticed for promotion or recognition.

There is nothing more liberating than the feeling that you are loved for who you are and someone accepts and embraces your faults. Give others a chance to get to know and love who you truly are!

HOW TO BECOME AN INSPIRATION TO OTHERS

Many people are unable to inspire others because they don't consider the precious qualities and skills they have and can share. Instead, they try to draw as much attention to themselves as possible. They merely display themselves as cheap celebrities! For some people, it doesn't matter why, only that as many people as possible become their fans, follow them or love them! These people will do anything to impress other people, even if it has nothing to do with their true personality.

This approach is completely wrong!

You shouldn't aim for simply drawing attention to yourself. Show the world your personality and precious qualities, then people will naturally be drawn to you. Even if your goal is to make a name for yourself and to become well-known, you shouldn't cheapen yourself by not being genuine. Instead, strive to find the channel where you can reach the people who can elevate themselves through your uniqueness and precious skills! Nowadays, it is easy to get a lot of followers by putting on a mask and flaunting yourself. But since there are no real values or authenticity behind this, you can't be a real inspiration to others. If people don't follow you for your personality, and rather only for the pretty pictures or videos, you can easily be replaced by someone else. Although you may get results that way, they won't last!

This same mistake can occur on a date if you show no personality at all and merely rely on your beauty, hiding the special, unique traits that you have. When this happens, you shouldn't be surprised that a man you thought you connected with leaves for another beautiful *and* charismatic woman.

I believe that everyone is special, but many people are unaware of what makes them unique, so they are unable to express it to others. The inspiration level is about helping others by using and expressing your best qualities. If you are a great listener, then listen to others. If you cook delicious dishes, then uplift others' lives by doing just that!

Show people your beliefs, loves, passions and reasons to get up in the morning. This could be sharing anything from a great recipe for pancakes, to the perfect trick to make your laundry smell amazing. Share something that you feel called to share, something you truly believe can help make people around you feel better and happier. I am convinced that there are people out there who will love who you truly are, your real self, and will appreciate your unique qualities. Inspiration is about giving and giving is one of the greatest joys in life. Through giving, both parties win—the giver and the receiver!

After about 20 years together, I asked my husband what it is he adores so much about me. Throughout all the years we've spent together, he always told me that he couldn't imagine being with anyone else. Do you know what his reply was?

"I believe you inspire me perfectly because you are able to bring out of me what I wish to bring out of myself. I love that you truly believe in me, even if sometimes you nag or criticize me. I love the way you encourage me to succeed and praise my accomplishments in the very areas I want to develop and succeed in too.

Just like you, I love the challenge of building a business and going through the entrepreneurial journey. Being an entrepreneur takes up a huge chunk of my day-to-day life. It would be terrible if I had to build my business with someone by my side who detested this journey, because I would feel unsupported, unappreciated and misunderstood. There would be no one to cheer me on (and sometimes bug me) to take steps in the right direction. If you were different, you might hold me back, hamper me or suffocate me. But you *are* this way, and I love that you inspire me, cheer me on and bring out the person I aspire to become."

I hope now you understand that you can reach the maximum level of attractiveness by inspiring others through who you truly are!

Real Attractiveness and magnetism lie within being yourself!

BONUS TIP

Having an impact on others makes you charismatic, but so does allowing people to have an impact on you! An interesting social psychology experiment was conducted on this subject.[81] They examined whom people found the most attractive at the end of a date. In the first phase of the experiment, the subjects invite people on a date, and are instructed to agree with everything the other person said. In the second phase of the experiment, the subjects

---

81 "The Psychology of Seduction | Raj Persaud | TEDxUniversityofBristol," Tedx Talks, YouTube, July 7, 2016, https://www.youtube.com/watch?v=3E46oWB4V0s.

are instructed to disagree with everything the other person says. Lastly, in the third case, subjects are instructed to spend the first half of the date disagreeing with everything the other person says, and then agree with them during the second half.

Unsurprisingly, the subjects were found the least attractive when they disagreed with everything the other person said. What was surprising is that, regardless of physical appearance, the subject was found to be most attractive when they disagreed during the first half of the date and then later began agreeing. The reason this person was viewed as more attractive was that the other person felt that they had had an impact on them, and being able to make an impact on someone made that person more interesting to them. Just think about making a joke! We love it when someone else makes us laugh with their jokes, but not only that, we love it when we can get a good laugh out of them with our own jokes too!

chapter seven

LET'S TALK ABOUT SEX...

A NOTE ON L.O.R.A. AND SEXUAL ATTRACTIVENESS

Throughout the process of writing this book, I wanted to challenge my own convictions. With each statement, I would consider every possible argument against it. Whenever I managed to find a convincing objection, I eliminated the original statement. I also used this process in developing the Levels of Real Attractiveness (L.o.R.A.). The completed L.o.R.A. system went through a lot of refining to ensure that I was giving you something that would hold up in every respect!

When I developed the levels system, I considered the possibility of a person failing to develop their charisma and magnetism. If failure was indeed possible, despite completing all the levels, I considered the reasons for that failure.

This is how I concluded that, while discussing attractiveness, I absolutely needed to dedicate special attention to sex appeal and how to accentuate it. I have realized that there can be a scenario where a woman is pretty, kind, open, self-confident, balanced, continually developing herself and inspiring others, but despite all that, they still don't attract the opposite sex or a desirable partner. And for one very simple reason. They have no sex appeal! They may be beautiful, kind and intelligent, but somehow don't turn others on. An example of this is when men say a woman is cute, but they don't see her as a potential partner because she is more like a buddy to them. They put her in the "friend zone."

This is exactly why I need to talk about this in a separate, dedicated chapter. When writing about attractiveness, sexual appeal cannot go unmentioned!

Everything we have discussed so far will form the basis of your personal charisma, which is why it is truly indispensable that you learn and acquire these levels. Consider this chapter more like an optional module, which gives you a little extra on top of the basics. There are some techniques that are necessary if you want to attract a desirable partner with your sexual attractiveness!

WHAT DOES IT TAKE TO SEXUALLY AROUSE THE OPPOSITE SEX?

When sexual attraction develops between two parties, a flame of passion ignites. Both sides must nurture this flame to keep it burning over time.

First, let's take a look at ourselves, because if we are not comfortable with ourselves, then it will be impossible for us to unlock the full potential of our own sexual appeal! To have powerful sex appeal, it is essential that you are comfortable with your own body and femininity. Enjoy who you are and do not suppress the wonderful and mysterious world of your femininity! Anyone who has gone through the various levels of L.o.R.A. and has performed the exercises provided in each chapter won't have any difficulty with this.

The physical feature that attracts men the most is the 70%[82] waist–hip ratio.[83] There are evolutionary reasons for this, since wide hips represent fertility. It is a biological, instinctive trait that men look for in women. Try to choose your outfit to give your figure an effect as near to this proportion as possible.

Dressing for sexual attractiveness is a balancing act. Wearing overly skimpy, revealing clothes may make you appear less classy. But showing too little skin may put you solidly in the "friend zone." The key to this usually lies in the little, subtle details, such as lace tights or some other special detail in the outfit. It's a much more polished and effective way of dressing sexily. You must learn what your best assets are and accentuate those features. If you have

82 Eric W. Dolan, "Study: Men Remember More About a Woman with an 'Optimal' Waist-to-Hip Ratio," PsyPost, November 27, 2016, https://www.psypost.org/2016/11/study-men-remember-woman-optimal-waist-hip-ratio-46101.

83 The waist-to-hip ratio (WHR): 0.7. This value is calculated by dividing the waist circumference by the hip circumference. Example: Dividing 63 cm of waist circumference by 90 cm of hip circumference makes 0.7.

beautiful long legs, don't be afraid of shorter skirts, but balance it out with a top with more coverage. If your cleavage is beautiful, accentuate that feature, but not by putting everything on display.

Color choices also play a part. Warm colors have a more seductive quality and will make you appear more open, so choose them over other colors. It is hard not to be seductive when you're dressed in red!

Get ready every day as if you were getting ready for a hot date! Put on perfume, shave and wear sexy lingerie or no lingerie at all. This is not about other people. No one else needs to know about it; it is enough if you know! This is about changing your behavior to influence your sex appeal. When you do things that make you feel sexy, that energy is picked up on by the people around you. It also increases your confidence and puts you in the right mood to attract sexual or romantic partners.

I know that if you haven't done this before, it will seem intimidating at first, but trust me, it is a question of creating a habit. It's like brushing your teeth. If you pay attention to it every day for a month, then it will become a normal activity.

EXERCISES

Buy yourself sexy lingerie, and use it every day, regardless of whether you have a date that day or not! Or even wear nothing at all!

✿

Shave so you can have baby soft skin all the time!

✂

When you put on your perfume in the morning, spray some on your wrists. Close your eyes and lift your wrist to your nose, and slowly, deeply inhale its fragrance. Feel how irresistible it has made you!

Very important: for sex appeal, it is indispensable that you are happy, optimistic, and you exude the sense that you enjoy your life to the fullest! Be able to have a laid-back demeanor; don't take life too seriously, and let yourself have a good, hearty laugh whenever you can.

AWAKEN YOUR SENSUALITY

It's important to awaken your sensuality, but how can you do that?

Tune your senses. Put some sensual perfume on your wrist, close your eyes, and enjoy the scent. Put on sensual music, close your eyes, and feel it in your every cell. My personal favorite is Madonna's song, "Justify My Love."

Feel free to be naked as often as possible when you are alone. Feel and accept who you are, enjoy the way you look and don't worry about flaws. Be confident about your own body, femininity and self. See how wonderful you are. Let yourself be in your own naked reality.

Dance and roll your hips to get your blood pumping, especially when you're naked. It works in clothes too, which is exactly what we do in Beautyrobic classes, and many thousands of women are proof of it.

Love, enjoy, kiss, hug—because she who loves and is loved glows. If you don't have a partner, you can still draw sensual energy out of yourself. It's very important to learn to love yourself and to be kind and considerate with yourself and your body (see: K.O. level). Don't be afraid to love and touch yourself. It's no accident that we include as much body caressing as we can to Beautyrobic exercises. It works! Feel and enjoy touching and stroking your body. And if you are at home alone, you can go even further. Don't miss touching your breasts and genitals. Listen to your body and give yourself pleasure. This is very important.

Perform the previously mentioned shower ritual and breathing ritual every day.

Try Meditattractiveness. Practice it every day for a month and measure its effectiveness. If it works, do it every single day. Do it in style: dim the lights, light a candle, start a diffuser and put on some sexy lingerie. Start your day like this and you will see what a great impact it has on your life.

Try adult toys. Today, there are so many tools and ways to discover your own sexuality. Don't be afraid to try them. Sex shops offer plenty of tools to help you discover yourself. Get to know the options and try whatever piques your curiosity. Let go of expectations. Do everything at a pace that is good for you. Life is too short, I say, so enjoy it! Let's play!

THE ART OF FLIRTING

If you want people to open up and flirt with you, there is one thing you absolutely need to remember from this chapter. Men flirt with women who they can tell are open to it. They don't usually approach or try to get to know women who seem angry, bitter or negative. If you are getting in touch with your sex appeal and want to attract a sexual or romantic partner, it won't work unless you are open to it. I spoke to many male colleagues and friends of mine. They all agreed that if a woman appears approachable, both visually and with the aura she gives off, they are far more likely to approach her and attempt flirting than if she seems cold and closed off. When you want to flirt and be flirted with, make sure the men around you are aware of that. This doesn't mean, of course, that you should give yourself away too easily…!

I'D LIKE TO SHARE WITH YOU THE MOST IMPORTANT THINGS TO KNOW ABOUT FLIRTING.

1. **Smile.** Keep in mind that a negative, angry or stand-offish woman is unappealing. If a man attempts to flirt with you and you react in a disinterested and uppity manner, you can bet that he'll stop his approach for good! A man won't go anywhere near even the most beautiful woman if she behaves in an arrogant manner with other people. And so, if your goal is to repel, then this could be a useful tool to achieve it. But if you want your crush to start flirting with you, then smile at him, be laid-back and exude happiness. This is yet another reason why it's worthwhile to work at

the various levels of L.o.R.A.! Of course, a smile is not the same thing as giggling.

2. **Don't leave your sense of humor at home.** Research has shown that a great sense of humor is very important when it comes to seduction![84] But humor means different things to men and women. Women adore men who have a great sense of humor, and men adore women who get their jokes and laugh at them! So, if you want a man to go crazy about you, appreciate his jokes.

3. **Praise.** Thank him whenever he is courteous to you and appreciate it if he pays you compliments. When he sees that he can make a positive impact on you, he will become even more courteous and attentive towards you and pay you even more compliments.

4. **Look deeply in his eyes.** As they say, the eyes are the window to the soul! When you want to seduce someone, look deeply into his eyes. If you can't maintain eye contact for too long, look down and then look up again and reestablish the eye contact.

5. **Play with your hair and use tiny movements to touch it.** This is not only very feminine, but very sexy too.

6. **Tease.** Don't just nod in agreement like a bobble-head doll! Disagree with him with a playful tone. Doing this

---

84 Christine Metz Howard, "Laughter, Then Love: Study Explores Why Humor is Important in Romantic Attraction," The University of Kansas, September 2, 2015, https://news.ku.edu/2015/08/27/first-comes-laughter-then-love-study-finds-out-why-humor-important-romantic-attraction.

will make him fight even harder to make an impact on you!

7. **Touch.** Touch him, but not too obviously, and not all the time. It also matters where you touch him. If you don't want to appear too clingy, just touch him lightly on his arm.

8. **Let him be the man.** Throughout the process of human evolution, men have played the role of the hunter and protector. Let him do his job now too. Be the woman by his side that he needs to protect.

9. **Make him feel special and sexy!** Remember when I told you people long to be near those who make them feel special? Give him special attention, but don't be over the top. Just show him that you are interested, and that you find him sexy and special!

10. **When you're flirting with him, make sure he feels that he will need to fight for you!** When he feels like he has got you and you are wrapped around his finger, his chasing instinct diminishes, and he will lose interest in trying to make an impact on you!

FLIRTING HAS THREE PHASES, AND THE LIMITS OF EACH ARE DISTINCTLY DIFFERENT!

1. At the very beginning, the two of you are flirting very cautiously and delicately. It is important that he knows you are interested but not that you are crazy about him. He should not be sure about your level of your interest.

2. When it has become obvious that you are into each other and you both clearly want more, then show him that you like him. But remember, he must not see that you are crazy about him, because that would put an end to his chasing instinct!

3. The sexual flirt! This works when things have escalated, either when you have already hooked up, or when the sexual heat in the air between you has reached high intensity. At this point, your flirting can be very hot and obvious, but you may want to be careful that no one else can hear, otherwise someone could easily consider you too forward!

THE PERFECT DATE

When you're on a date, all you have to do is to practice the things you have learned so far and your success will be guaranteed! A perfect date is one that is playful and laid-back, and you can have fun in each other's company and laugh a lot. The two of you should be flirting with each other during practically the whole date. Follow the steps of flirting and most importantly, be yourself! Anyone who has gone through the steps in this book and has got to this point will be interesting company, whether she's on a date or with a group of friends.

A TIP FOR THE DATE

Make sure that external circumstances and stimuli never disturb the time and attention you are about to dedicate to each other. If you can pick the location of the date, choose one that makes you feel good. Put on an outfit that you are comfortable in and create the perfect circumstance for you with your environment.

The last thing you want is to be constantly worrying about where your favorite dress cuts into your flesh, whether your roots are showing and so on. It goes without saying that you shouldn't forget the tips I gave you earlier. Look your best but don't prioritize sporting a sexy outfit over your comfort. If you feel good in what you're wearing, it will show! There is nothing worse than when a woman doesn't know how to walk in heels or is fidgeting with her outfit because it doesn't fit her or makes her feel uncomfortable. You shouldn't feel pressured to wear anything because you think you must go over the top to be attractive!

Ultimately, the date should allow you both to be as comfortable as possible, be your authentic selves and have a great time in each other's company. If both of you succeed in putting your best foot forward, sooner or later, that may lead to sex…

THE L.O.R.A. SYSTEM, WHEN IT COMES TO SEX…

The levels of L.o.R.A. can be perfectly applied to sex.
Just think about it:

Level 1 Appearance

When you get to the point that you are finally ready to make love with your crush for the first time and you strip off your clothes, it is a fantastic feeling when your partner sees a desirable, well-groomed sweet-smelling woman who is mind-blowingly sexy, regardless of whether she's wearing lingerie or nothing but perfume. The first level of L.o.R.A. will give you exactly this!

Level 2 K.O. = Kindness and Openness

Once you have the sexy appearance, it's time for the second level of L.o.R.A. A woman who reaches the second level is open, kind, receptive and pays attention to her partner and his needs, including sexually. By reaching the second level, she will be open to new things and won't shy away when her partner shows her something new. She pays attention to what her partner likes and what gives him pleasure. See how the positive effect of L.o.R.A. can come in handy in the bedroom too?

Level 3 Self-Confidence

Let's go one step further. When a woman has learned to master the third level of L.o.R.A., she is self-confident in the bedroom too. She doesn't hide herself or cover up her body. She can be truly relaxed, which allows her to concentrate on her partner and her own pleasure. She's not obsessing about how she might look from behind, or how much her love handles show, or what her partner will say when he sees them!

Level 4 B.A.G. = Balance, Awareness, Growth

When a woman has learned the fourth level of L.o.R.A., she is in perfect harmony with herself, knows herself and her body and can live in her femininity. She also knows exactly what makes her happy in the bedroom, how she can be satisfied and what she wants in bed. At the same time, she is open to evolving constantly and willing to experiment, explore and learn new things too!

Level 5 Inspiration

Finally, imagine the woman who has learned the first four levels perfectly. She looks great and is sexy, kind, open to other people and pays attention to their needs. She is also confident, doesn't hide her body, and has the courage to be open and to live in the present moment. She's sure of herself and loves herself. She knows what she needs and wants sexually, is open to constant improvement and possesses the highest level of sexual attractiveness. She is able to inspire other people. She knows one thing—she knows how to knock men off their feet!

I believe that such a woman will have a devoted fan for life because, after all of that, a man won't want anyone else! There's a saying that expresses this concept perfectly: "A woman's looks can captivate you, her soul can seize you, but good sex will chain you to her forever." Regarding men, I've got to say it couldn't be truer! All you need to do is to follow all the steps I have taught you in this book and transfer them over to the level of your sex life too.

HOW DOES THIS WORK IN PRACTICE?

The thing is, it's all in your mind, and that's true for the bedroom too! If you complete the exercises in this book one by one, your perspective will change. In the bedroom, there are certain techniques that a woman can only learn in practice; you just need to be open to them and then practice them.

A relationship that gives sexual pleasure depends on both partners, which is why it's impossible to give you one-size-fits-all advice. What turns one person on could be a turn-off for someone else. Every couple must become synchronized. You and your partner need to talk about your erotic experiences and sexual desires honestly. Before you can talk about it openly, you must know exactly what you want, and for that, you have to know yourself, your body and your needs! The more we learn to communicate with our partner openly about what we need—and not just sexually—the stronger and more connected our relationships will grow to be. The more connected the couple, the better the sex.

There was a study about this phenomenon, where scientists examined whether the length of time men and women were in a relationship influenced their levels of sexual desire.[85] In other words, whether couples had more satisfying sex lives when they had been together for a short time or when they had been together for a long time. They hypothesized that people would experience a higher level of sexual desire when they entered into a new romantic relationship, but they discovered that the latter group actually had greater sexual satisfaction.[86] So, in fact, the best thing couples can do to have a happy relationship and satisfying sex life for the long haul is to build up and constantly nurture their relationship. The ability to communicate their emotions and desires honestly and openly to their partners requires them to understand themselves first. This again demonstrates the immense importance of adequate self-awareness and the B.A.G. level in our lives.

I find it necessary to mention that there can be many factors preventing someone from experiencing pleasure from sexual activity. This could stem from physical or medical conditions (e.g., painful intercourse) or past psychological trauma. Whatever the case, this would exceed the scope of this book. If you are struggling with either, don't ignore it. You must work through it and consult

---

85 Mario Mikulincer and Phillip R. Shaver, *Attachment in Adulthood: Structure, Dynamics, and Change* (New York: Guilford Press, 2016).

86 Ibid.

with a professional if needed. Solving these problems may require therapy, either individual or couples, or the help of a medical doctor. If you don't address this, all other measures you take will be wasted because you will be unable to make progress.

REGULARITY

I like to equate sex to eating chocolate! If you don't have it for a long time, you stop craving it as much. While in the case of eating chocolate, restraint may be a positive thing, going without sex for a long time has a lot of negative consequences for our health overall.

People who have sex regularly are less prone to high blood pressure and heart attacks.[87] Regular sex for women is attributed to avoiding urinary incontinence issues and strengthens the immune system.[88] Sexual activity has serious benefits in regulating mood, as it is a great stress reliever and feel-good hormones are released at climax, including endorphins, oxytocin and dopamine.[89] Additionally, passionate lovemaking increases blood flow, circulation and boosts metabolism too, meaning that it can help to make us feel even more attractive.[90]

But we are not going to examine the benefits of sex from a medical perspective in detail. Ultimately, being deprived of sex for long periods of time has a negative consequence that is connected to our topic. If you neglect this need of your body and soul and let it go unsatisfied, it will negatively impact your energy and glow.

87 Kara Mayer Robinson, "10 Surprising Health Benefits of Sex," WebMD, March 6, 2022, https://www.webmd.com/sex-relationships/guide/sex-and-health.

88 Ibid.

89 Ibid.

90 Ibid.

There is something sexy and sexually attractive about the energy of a woman who has regular sex, which is something men can perceive unconsciously. An example of this is when you want to have a man in your life, but there isn't a single guy showing any interest. No matter how glammed up you get or how perfect your makeup may be, men just don't notice you in the way you want to be noticed. Then, suddenly, you find someone and end up in an exclusive, committed relationship. The two of you are happy and sexually satisfied and suddenly you notice a complete shift. Men begin hitting on you all of a sudden! They seem to want you like never before, even when you're not particularly dressed up. This shift comes from a change that occurs in your energy and glow, which men can unconsciously detect. So often, I have heard my girlfriends complain, "Why do all the men want me more now, once I have a boyfriend? Where were they when I was single???"

I know that this can be a delicate subject, but you mustn't let the sexual fire within you die completely. Even if you don't have a partner, don't neglect your own body! Regular masturbation may help you achieve this, even without a partner. Pleasuring yourself will also allow you to explore your body and learn what makes you feel good! The more frequently you pleasure yourself, the more you will get to know your own sexual needs, which will have an impact on your sex life and your sexual energy too. Most people tend to avoid this subject, but it will still influence you, so you *must* analyze and address it. Dedicate time to studying this area and explore what gives you pleasure!

My advice to anyone who feels uncomfortable talking about masturbation is to consider the underlying reasons behind it. If you can't address this on your own, you may want to consult. an expert. In many families, the topic of sex is taboo. Many parents are too embarrassed or don't know how to talk about it with their children. If a person is taught from a very young age that sexuality is something to be ashamed of, that could be a recipe for an unhappy sex life. Remember, the suppression and denial of sexual needs may lead to negative effects on your health, both physically and mentally—not to mention the fact that an unsatisfying sex life will have a terrible impact on your sexual and feminine energy. So, I hope I have now convinced you that this indeed is something to address!

EXERCISE

Try out something new sexually every month! If you are single, experiment on yourself. If you have a partner, do it with them. Then observe the types of changes you experience.

TRY MEDITATTRACTIVENESS

Throughout my career, I realized that the biggest challenge for women is not finding practical advice on how to look their best, it is developing their inner fire, strong charisma and an inner passion that will make them truly, spiritually attractive.

One of the many reasons I adore Beautyrobic is because I can see the transformation, week by week, in the women using the program. The transformation is not only physical but also spiritual, in terms of inner feminine energy. Meditattractiveness is a special and complex sequence of exercises geared towards making women their most attractive and irresistible selves and enabling them to accept and love who they see in the mirror. Its specific exercises have a targeted effect on attractiveness and increase the inner fire within! You can do the exercises in your own home, with no special equipment, and make them part of your daily routine. It is important to use techniques and exercises like Meditattractiveness that are targeted towards increasing your feminine energy and inner fire.

CLOSING REMARKS

I have a very important, final comment that I hope will help you achieve the same results as I did: **maximizing your glow does not mean being perfect at each Level of Real Attractiveness**. I'm not perfect at all and nor do I want to be. You can't afford to be an expert in everything and if you care about everything and everyone around you, you won't have time for yourself. Relaxation and "me time" are essential to your attractiveness and glow. Remember the B.A.G. level.

But if you really want to be attractive and glow inside and out, you have to work on yourself until you reach the critical point in each level of L.o.R.A. where it is no longer an obstacle to your attractiveness. Let me give you an example:

In Level 1, it's all about the looks. I ask you to take care of your body, but this is not to say that you will only be attractive if you have a six pack. Simply make sure you live in a healthy body that is in harmony with your self-image, self-esteem and desires!

Although you do have to dedicate some time out of your busy lifestyle to these steps, I don't want you to feel discouraged or think that you need to give them your undivided attention or won't be able to squeeze it into your life. You may well know that the best things in life don't come easy to us. If you feel this is too much at first and you are unable to do it, please do not give up! Remember: Rome wasn't built in a day, so give yourself some time to achieve the results you're looking for. As you start working on one level at a time, you will begin to experience the positive changes in your life. The good news is that even a small change can make a huge difference in your life and will give you the strength to continue to grow.

Don't overthink it. Just get started, follow the steps, and enjoy the results!

GET THE MOST OUT OF THIS BOOK—GIFT FOR YOU

WHAT IS THE NEXT STEP?

I've been coaching women for more than a decade now. I took about a year and a half to write this book because I wanted to publish a comprehensive discussion on the subject and a complex system based on research.

To provide a broad view, I interviewed experts who have demonstrated outstanding results in their fields. I also included exercises at the end of the chapters that will help you develop a deeper understanding of the different levels of the L.o.R.A. system.

I want to give you something real that will strongly impact your life. For this, you need to build an everyday habit to maintain and improve your personal magnetism and attractiveness. I want you to experience your feminine magnetic power every single day. I want you to become a Mindful Magnetic Woman.

So, now I will give you a practical method that will not only boost the effect of this book but help you feel more balanced and glow inside and out.

BEAUTYROBIC—MAXIMIZE YOUR INNER AND OUTER GLOW

I have mentioned Beautyrobic in this book many times. This is because there are thousands of women who have attended classes or tried our programs online in the last decade who act as proof that it works. Beautyrobic helps to change women's lives and ensure health, beauty, femininity and success by building self-awareness and confidence both physically and mentally. Beautyrobic introduces you to a world where you can learn to accept and love yourself and focus on developing your own unique values instead of copying other people's.

The Beautyrobic concept consists of Beautyrobic workout programs that use specific moves designed for women mixed with a hardcore strength workout and stretching at the end. Beautyrobic fitness programs involve a mixture of effective fat burning, interval and strength training, and stretching spiced with special feminine moves. Because there is no choreography, anyone can join at any time and at any level. The workout programs complement each other, providing a complex workout that strengthens and shapes the body, improves women's health, gives a lean and beautiful look, prevents injuries and helps relaxation. As a result, participants can build confidence and a positive attitude, which contributes to becoming happy and successful in every aspect of their life.

Beautyrobic, besides being a hardcore workout, places a lot of emphasis on femininity and the attractiveness of women by becoming self-aware and confident, both physically and mentally. Besides the fitness programs, Beautyrobic provides other special programs and tutorials to improve women's health and confidence. The programs are supported by the expertise of psychologists and physiotherapists to ensure their safety and effectiveness.

Beautyrobic helps to satisfy women's physical and mental needs while enhancing their beauty, and I want you to experience the feeling of inner and outer glow. Let me help you to take the first step towards your feminine magnetism. Let me help you to become a Mindful Magnetic Woman. I believe in the power of daily habits, so I would like to give you a special gift that you can factor into your daily life and begin to feel the miracle of this whole concept.

Please visit the website for your gift
www.mindfulmagneticwoman.com/gift
From Brigitta, with love.

DON'T JUST TAKE
MY WORD FOR IT.

BEAUTYROBIC REVIEWS

"It seems like such a long time ago and it's shocking to look back at myself. Not so much because of my appearance, but rather because I see a picture of an anxious woman with low self – esteem. It was around the time when my daughter turned 1… I was functioning so much as a mother that I couldn't see traces of a WOMAN anymore when looking in the mirror. " I was looking for a workout that would fill me inside, and that wasn't about my body, but about me and my femininity.

At Beautyrobic, I felt an indescribable FEMININITY that I missed, like deserts miss the rain. I started to open up very slowly and fell in love with myself. And the most amazing feeling was that my environment noticed that too. I became a better mother and my husband started to see the WOMAN in me again.

It cannot be put into words how it felt when I found the kind of ME-TIME that simultaneously gave my body fitness, health to my soul and a maximum charge to MY FEMININITY! 🖤"

—CSILLA TORONYI-MOLNAR

"I've become more confident. Before I've always been waiting for confirmation from men and relationships that I'm a real, sexy woman. Of course it's very important for a woman to hear that from her partner, but now I can believe that that's right and I'm not just waiting for outside confirmations. What else I've got from Beautyrobic is that I dare to dream, and if we really want something and do something getting it is all possible. Thank you for dreaming and making Beautyrobic for us!"

—GEORGINA

"Beautyrobic is really not just a workout, it doesn't only shape women's looks, but also their personalities and self-esteem. It's a real "glow up" workout. Nothing can improve my mood and self-image so much and so quickly like Beautyrobic. I'm doing myself a favor and I'm still feeling good in the process. I don't think I could ask for more."

—ZSOFI SZABO

"Beautyrobic is simply the perfect combination, an ingenious workout mix of greatly structured, very effective and enjoyable, feminine movements. It's a kind of spiritual recharge, a gradual relaxation for those who are more rigid in this field. As for the long run, it's really addictive: on the one hand because it's amazingly spectacular: a great shape is guaranteed in 2-3 hours a week, very quickly. But more importantly, it has a spiritual, mental impact. It releases, relaxes, and gives a lot of energy' It's worth more than any psychologist or mood enhancer."

—EMESE

"My story started about 7 years ago. I didn't exercise at all during university and work, I ate a lot and just snacked all day. It showed: I gained a lot of weight (over 20kg) I become 75kg and a sizl2... Finally, 3 years ago I first met Beautyrobic, which didn't only change my appearance, but constantly filled me up with positive energy, which made me more confident, brave and girly. Comfortable jeans, skirts and high heels moved into my wardrobe while I was getting more and more compliments from those around me. The slow and persistent work paid off: I lost 25 kgs and 4 dress sizes with Beautyrobic. My waist got thinner than when I was 18, and my bottom and thighs became shaped, which I don't have to cover up in a swimsuit either.

And meanwhile I became a Beautyrobic instructor, wife and mom." 🖤

—VERONIKA MARKUS

"So after almost 1 year of hard work my time has also come to thank you for creating Beautyrobic, with which I twerked, rolled, planked and shook off 10 kg (20 pounds). For me, Beautyrobic is no longer just a form of workout, but a PASSION (in capital letters) and the essence of femininity in the most classical sense. I ventured to my first class when everything around me collapsed, but I can only see it now, that in fact, that's when everything actually clicked. Thank you very much!" 🖤

—NOEMI NEMETH

"I've tried a lot of workouts before, but I always missed something. Although I never knew, and I still don't know what it was, it sure is in Beautyrobic.

Beautyrobic nurtures body and soul at the same time. I fell in love with it and it only got stronger as I got to know more moves, individual mixes, and different instructors. I like morning workouts the most. If I start the day with Beautyrobic, it can only be good. If for some reason I have to skip it, I miss it. I think I became a Beautyrobic addict from the first time.

As a model, I always have to be in perfect shape. With Beautyrobic, I can keep myself in perfect shape. I think this is the most ideal form of training for every woman."

—YASMIN EISAM ELDEEN

"I finally started to like myself, have a feminine body and the best is: I feel sexy!"

—BOGI

"Yes! Beautyrobic led me back to myself! My relationship has been improved because I feel like a woman again! And it has positive impacts in all areas of my life!"

—ROZALIA

Beautyrobic through the eyes of a psychologist

—EXCERPT FROM THE WRITING OF PSYCHOLOGIST AND BEAUTYROBIC GUEST MIHAELA NISTOR 🖤

"Beautyrobic helps us to confidently accept, love, and praise our body. By doing this, our relationship with our own body also changes. As we learn to accept ourselves and our bodies (whatever they may be like), we are greatly helping initiating external and internal change and achieving the desired shape. Another positive effect of Beautyrobic is that it helps strengthen women's self-confidence.

Why is the way you see yourself when you look in the mirror important? It really does matter, whether you see yourself as Miss Nobody or a real Diva. No matter how you feel about yourself or your body, a stranger will immediately perceive it. Because you project this inner image of yourself outward, that is, how you "carry yourself." I think Beautyrobic can make a big difference in this area too. A woman who has learned to "carry herself" and is aware of what message she conveys non-verbally can be very attractive to everyone. I think Beautyrobic's success also lies in the fact that while we go through really, sexy, sensual practices and discover the goddess that lives within us – meaning our own femininity - in the long run it radiates with a strong self-confidence that can be very appealing to the environment. This self-confidence and self-esteem will surely be picked up on very quickly by the other sex, because there is nothing more beautiful, than a woman with healthy self-confidence."

—MIHAELA NISTOR

"Beautyrobic will not only give you a gorgeous body, but it will also enable you to stay focused on remaining a real woman in today's challenging and ever-changing world."

—DORI CSIZMEG

"Even though our lives are far away now, I got an immeasurable amount of help from you when I needed it most. Thanks to you I regained my feminine self-confidence, and if that wasn't enough, you stood before us as the most inspiring role model to this day. When I started going to your classes, I wanted to be like Brigitta Békési. Then you taught me how to be me (Ági Fischl). And I won't forget that."

—AGI FISCHL

"Beautyrobic has given me a form of training that I would recommend to anyone in a heartbeat. It gave me self-confidence, faith and a new career as well. A new role model and new mentors too. Brigitta Békési = WW Brigi (I only call her Wonder Woman Brigi because that's who she is) expanded my comfort zone to such a level that I would have never thought. I learned to squat properly, which I never knew because of competitive dancing, and the shape of my ass is also developing (Body). It took me about a year and a half to become a Beautyrobic instructor. I started to have goals! I learned to wait and see that nothing comes to us right away (Mind). My new posture and radiance was noticed by the men around me and also by the unknown (Beauty). I still have to practice a lot (especially the charisma of kindness :) but the Wow Effect really works. The isolations and the hip rolls (plus a pinch of Meditattractiveness) completely transformed my sex life too. I don't settle for anything less than the best anymore and I dare to bring it on! I can't even imagine what else awaits me here. Thank you Beautyrobic! Thank you Brigi! "

—ZSUZSI LASZLO

"My self-confidence increased. What you give makes our lives so much better.

I have never had so much confidence in myself!"

—ESZTER

"The exercises helped me to be able to connect to my feminine energy, and over the past year I've received more compliments than I've ever received in my life, even though I've always took care of myself."

—TIMI

"By doing Beautyrobic, we transform an amazing force and resource consciousness and easily accessible and turn it into some kind of proudness. I love the way that I can almost touch that inexplicable awesomeness that is part of every class and all of a sudden we all become women of doom.

And it's there in all of us, we just have to lure it out. :) Well, that's why I've been doing Beautyrobic for almost 5 years now."

—DORCI

"I first attended Beautyrobic in January, 2016 and immediately fell in love with it. I felt like it became a part of my life right away. Thanks to Beautyrobic I finally started to workout regularly.

The workout itself is all about feminine movements, you have to pay attention to every single movement to be feminine. This makes it harder and more effective. I felt the effect after just a month of regular Beautyrobic: my posture got better, I became more confident, and got my first praise for my tighter bottom (that's exactly what I didn't expect). :) Since then, I have been constantly experiencing positive changes; the charming, beautiful radiance, the confidence, the beautiful, tight body, just to name a few. These are the results that can be expected from doing Beautyrobic :) During training, all participants are being beautified. :) The typical Beautyrobic movements and the joy make everyone beautiful, no matter how much they sweat :) Beautyrobic beautifies not only the body but also the soul and spirit!"

—SUSANNE

"I love every bit of Beautyrobic Home Pro! It's part of my everyday life, even if it's just 1 meditation with a face workout, but still. Not to mention the rest! I am more than before! I love you so much and you should be proud of yourself for helping so many women!"

—BETTINA

"I am determined to do the monthly program. I haven't finished yet but I can already feel the effect, I have more energy, and my inner goddess is awakening."

—SZLVIA

"What can I thank Beautyrobic for? I finally have a healthy self-confidence because I don't list my mistakes anymore, I look at myself in a completely different way in the mirror! The first picture of my life in a swimsuit that I don't say, Blah..." immediately as I see it and delete it not only from the camera but even from my memory in 'despair...

I'll never have the chopstick legs I have always wanted... that's not my genetics! But I finally don't mind! I accept my limits, it's me, but at the same time I do everything I can to make me feel good in my skin! And I see the result!

Feminine shapes, I absolutely feel like a real woman, during Beautyrobic and in many other areas of my life. Beautyrobic makes me free because it affects everything from a relationship to work! I highly recommend it to all women!"

—BOGI

"Beautyrobic emphasizes and strengthens individual femininity. So far, I have not come across such a form of training where femininity can be recharged by increasing your self-confidence."

—KINGA

Please visit the website for your gift
www.mindfulmagneticwoman.com/gift

ACKNOWLEDGEMENTS

First of all, I would like to thank the Beautyrobic girls because this book could not exist without them. Then I would like to thank my husband for his patience and support throughout the whole process. Sometimes I was hard to manage, but he always stood by me. I would like to thank my mentor Luigino Bottega for his creative ideas and useful advice. For the international publication, I want to give special thanks to Sriram Venkataraman for always encouraging and motivating me and to Lindsay Peragine of Key Lime Media LLC for her amazing help in the first edit of the English version. And thank you to Book Launchers for making my book available in English and supporting me when I felt lost.

Do you want to learn more about how to become the best version of a mindful magnetic woman of yourself?

@mindfulmagneticwoman

visit
BEAUTYROBIC.COM

@mindfulmagneticwoman

Beautyrobic.

Want to develop your confidence and femininity in practice not just to read about it?

Try Beautyrobic®'s special exercises anywhere, anytime, that work both inside and out to maximize your attractiveness and

Beautyrobic® Home Pro
Maximize Your Inner and Outer Glow

beautyrobic.com/beautyrobic-home-pro
Instagram: @beautyrobic_official
TikTok: @beautyrobic

Do you want to continue the journey towards maximizing Real Attractiveness? And in the comfort of your own home?

With the Beautyrobic® Home Pro subscription, you'll get access to a complex of special programs tailored for women that will improve your femininity, confidence and attractiveness, because they have a fantastic effect on all five levels of the L.O.R.A. system.

Check out how much is included!

Made in the USA
Monee, IL
20 July 2024

62379567R10122